Headlights on the Prairie

HEADLIGHTS

—— ON THE ——

PRAIRIE

Essays on Home

Robert Rebein

University Press of Kansas

Published by the University Press of Kansas (Lawrence, Kansas 66045), which was organized by the Kansas Board of Regents and is operated and funded by Emporia State University, Fort Hays State University, Kansas State University, Pittsburg State University, the University of Kansas, and Wichita State University.

Library of Congress Cataloging-in-Publication Data

Names: Rebein, Robert, 1964– author.
Title: Headlights on the prairie : essays on home / Robert Rebein.
Description: Lawrence : University Press of Kansas, [2017]
Identifiers: LCCN 2017020139 | ISBN 9780700624713 (paperback) |
ISBN 9780700624720 (ebook)
Subjects: LCSH: Rebein, Robert, 1964—Homes and haunts—Kansas. |
Kansas—Social life and customs. | Rebein, Robert, 1964—Childhood and youth. | Country life—Kansas—Anecdotes. | BISAC: HISTORY / United States / State & Local / Midwest (IA, IL, IN, KS, MI, MN, MO, ND, NE, OH, SD, WI).
Classification: LCC F686.2 .R43 2017 | DDC 978.1/76—dc23
LC record available at https://lccn.loc.gov/2017020139.

British Library Cataloguing-in-Publication Data is available.

Printed in the United States of America

10 9 8 7 6 5 4 3 2

The paper used in this publication is recycled and acid free and meets the minimum requirements of the American National Standard for Permanence of Paper for Printed Library Materials Z39.48-1992.

To Alyssa,
forever and always

Contents

—1—
Why I Hate *The Wizard of Oz*

Imagine having the land of your birth, a place about which you have complex and wildly ambivalent feelings, reduced to a black-and-white cartoon. Someone asks you where you're from, and when you reply "Kansas," this well-meaning stranger grins and blurts out, "Where's Toto? Oh, that's right. We're not in Kansas anymore!"

You get this in New York, Indiana, California. Even as far afield as Paris, you get it. "Kansoz! Ah, oui. Les munchkins!"

How to say you hail from a place uninhabited by tinmen and sweet little girls in pinafores, a demanding, starkly beautiful place with twenty-mile views, sunflowers as big as your head, and night skies so clear that you might believe yourself to have been born among stars? Where the wind blows without cease and flies bite like vampires and the stink of the slaughterhouse overhangs everything like a toxic cloud. Where it's not unusual for a kid like you to receive his first shotgun at ten, drive a wheat truck at twelve, and solo in a Beechcraft Debonair at fourteen or fifteen.

"Does that sound like Oz?" you want to ask.

But you don't. Why bother?

When the tornado came and swept you away, as you knew all along it would, it was not to drop you into some Technicolor fantasy, but rather into the same world of Applebee's and Best Buy the jokesters inhabit. That's the context here; that's the reason you refuse to join Dorothy's fan club.

—2—
Bullet in the Brain

One of my fourth-grade teachers, an ancient nun named Sister Urban, expressed concern about a tendency I had to "blank out" during class. One minute I'd be paying attention, but the next I'd be staring off into space, completely unresponsive. Twenty or thirty seconds might go by before the "episode" ended and I'd "return to consciousness," seemingly unaware that any of it had happened. Needless to say, it wasn't long before my mother dragged me off to see our family doctor, who examined me briefly before suggesting that I be seen by a specialist in Wichita, three hours away.

"Do you really think that's necessary?" my mother asked.

"Who knows?" Dr. Baum said, shrugging. "But in these kinds of cases, I'd say it's better to be safe than sorry."

In the days to come, the phrases *these kinds of cases* and *better safe than sorry* became a kind of mantra my mother repeated whenever she felt pressed to justify the trip—either to herself, to one of her neighborhood friends, or, most important, to my father, whose standard response to reports of illness or injury was some variation of "Hell, just look at him. There's nothing wrong with that kid."

As it happened, I agreed with my father's assessment. Deep in my bones, I knew I was okay. However, that didn't mean I was going to let an opportunity as sweet as this pass me by. The way I saw it, a trip with my mother to the big city of Wichita was bound to yield all manner of riches. At the very least, we'd get to eat lunch at McDonald's or Burger King (neither of which existed in Dodge City circa 1974), and should we happen to venture into a sporting goods store or, better yet, a *mall*, well, who could say what merchandise I might not talk her into buying me?

Although she spent many happy summers in the Flint Hills town of Maple Hill, my mother was born and raised in Wichita, where she moved after her mother married for the second time. In a way, you could say my mother had two diametrically opposed childhoods. In the first, she was the beloved only child of a single mother, with two sets of grandparents and various aunts and uncles playing a part in raising her. In the second, she was the much-older sister of four younger siblings, the youngest of whom, Scott, was born after she had left home to attend St. Mary of the Plains College in Dodge City. When my mother was still in her teens, her mother's health began to decline rapidly ("dropsy" and "women's troubles" were a couple of the terms doctors bandied about), and the result was that the younger kids in the family didn't have the same experiences or opportunities that she had while growing up. And the younger they were, the worse it had been. My mother felt guilty about this, but what could she do? She had her own life to live, and live it she must. In a way, that's what the town of Wichita came to mean to her. It was the scene of an escape, a necessary but bittersweet breaking away.

Our appointment was set for midmorning, so we had to leave the house at around 5 a.m. My father must have carried me to the car, because I remember nothing before I woke up in the back seat of our 1964 Impala wagon.

"How much longer?" I asked, rubbing my eyes.

"Not long now," my mother answered. "A little over an hour."

"Are we going to stop to eat?"

"I packed a breakfast for you," she said, smiling at me in the car's rearview mirror. "It's in that paper sack at your feet."

I pulled the bag onto the seat beside me and was disappointed to find it filled with apples, bananas, and other healthy things.

"What about after the appointment?" I asked. "Are we going to stop then?"

"We'll see," my mother answered, finishing a cigarette and tossing the butt out the car's window. It irked me how easily she evaded my attempts to get a promise on the books.

At the hospital, we had to wait an hour before it was my appointment time, and then another hour before the doctor was able to see me. My mother spent the time flipping through magazines while I ransacked the pay phones looking for change for the vending machines. I was conscious of everything—how big and sophisticated the hospital was, how the old and seriously ill were wheeled around on aluminum gurneys (beds on wheels!), how many of the patients and hospital workers were of a sort I'd never encountered before (I remember in particular a Hindu woman with a red dot on her forehead).

The doctor was a short man with wiry black hair. He spoke to me in flat, adult tones, with a minimum of the falsetto condescension I associated with doctors.

"What do you know about the test we're going to run today?"

"Nothing," I confessed.

"Well, it's called an EEG, and it's pretty simple. We're going to put some electrodes on your scalp. Those are to capture your brain waves. Once we've captured them, we're going to send them to San Francisco. Do you know where that is?"

"California."

"Right. And do you know *how* we're going to get your brain waves to California?"

I shook my head.

"Telephone wires. When you get back to school, you can tell your friends that your brain waves were sent to San Francisco via telephone wires."

"Does it hurt?" I asked.

"Not a bit."

I remember a dark room, blinking lights, the coolness of the cream they put on my skin, and the elaborate hooking up of the electrodes. The promised "call to California" was delayed several times before it finally went through. Then the lights came back on, and the nurses pulled the electrodes off one by one.

"When do we get the results?" my mother asked.

"The doctor will call you."

"That's it?"

"That's it," the nurse repeated.

Outside it was sunny and warm. It was lunch time, as nearly as I could tell. "Can we stop and get some food?" I asked. "Where are we going to eat? Can we go to McDonald's?"

"It's too early for lunch," my mother replied as we climbed into the Impala. "Have an apple if you're hungry."

Something had changed while I wasn't paying attention. In the hospital she'd been patient and upbeat, but now that the appointment was over, she'd become distracted and nervous. She gripped the steering wheel with both hands and leaned forward in her seat, as though trying to look through a dirty windshield. Having thrown one cigarette out the window, she promptly lit another. All of this was very unlike her.

"What's the matter?" I asked. "Don't you think the appointment went well?"

"It went fine."

"Well then?"

"Well, nothing," she answered irritably. "Stop bugging me and look out your window."

I did as I was told, noticing right away that the street we were on looked nothing like the ones we'd driven in on. Those streets had been busy and wide, full of stoplights and gas stations and fast-food restaurants. This street was smaller and shabbier, with weathered houses and ramshackle apartments on either side. Weeds grew up through cracks in the sidewalks, and some of the houses had cars and motorcycles parked in their beaten front yards. A couple of these cars were up on blocks, not a wheel or tire in sight. Dogs strained at the end of their chains, barking at us.

"Where are we?" I asked. "Did we make a wrong turn?"

"No, we didn't make a wrong turn."

"Are we lost?"

She shook her head. "We're just going to check on something. Then we'll be heading back home."

"Check on what?"

"Uncle Scott."

"Oh," I said.

Uncle Scott was my mother's youngest half-sibling. Born in 1952, he was only a couple of years older than my oldest brother. There were a lot of pictures in the family photo album in which Scott appeared alongside my brothers David, Alan, and Tom as just another shirtless, skinny kid posing against a backdrop of rolling plains. But in other ways, Scott was nothing at all like us. His mother, my grandmother Malinda, had died when Scott was nine years old, and his father, Guy, died five years after that. For a while, Uncle Scott's older brothers, my uncles Danny and Randy, took care of him. When that situation ran its course, Scott bounced around between the houses of various relatives in Kansas and Oklahoma. In 1969, after years of truancy, he dropped out of school for good, and not long after that, he received his draft notice. By 1971, at the age of nineteen, he was humping an M-16 through the jungles of South Vietnam.

My memories of Uncle Scott begin in the spring of 1973, when he stayed with us after returning home from the war. He was a thin, wiry dude with green, almost yellowish, eyes, curly brown hair, and a perpetual hangdog grin. Everything was funny to him in a dark, sarcastic way. He responded to news both good and bad with an understated laugh—*hee hee hee*—and a lazy shrug of the shoulders, as if to say, "Well, what do you expect?" This demeanor of his stood in stark contrast to the default mode of the rest of my family, which tended toward disciplined earnestness and a belief that everything would turn out all right if you just worked hard and followed the rules.

I remember one pheasant season—it must have been the Thanksgiving after Uncle Scott got back from Vietnam—when it was suggested to him (by my mother, no doubt) that he might enjoy going hunting with my brothers Alan and Tom, both of whom had recently taken up the sport.

"Of course, you'd need to buy a hunting license," Alan remarked, "and to get that, you'd need to have taken the Kansas Safe Hunter course."

Uncle Scott laughed. "Right. Hunter's safety. But how would they know if you *hadn't* taken the course?"

"You have to show them your card," Alan said.

"Well, just tell them you lost it, *hee hee hee.*"

"Yeah, but they'll ask for your number off the card," Alan said. "They have to put the number on your license."

"So you rattle one off. G152DOA74, *hee hee hee.* What could be easier than that?"

My brothers and I just sat there, looking at him. Needless to say, no pheasants were hunted that Thanksgiving weekend.

I was eight years old, that age when time is divided into big, uncomplicated categories like Halloween, Christmas, and Summer Vacation, when Uncle Scott came to stay with us. I watched cartoons every Saturday morning in order to keep up on the toys being offered as prizes in the different breakfast cereals. Then, on Saturday afternoons, I'd "help" my mother shop for food, locating all of the brands that had been advertised that morning and dragging them one by one to our cart.

"No," my mother would say, shaking her head firmly. "I already told you. We can't afford that one." Except that sometimes she relented. Perhaps three or four times a year, for reasons I could never understand or predict, she'd consent to the purchase of Cap'n Crunch or Lucky Charms or one of the other "expensive" brands. The Saturday before my Uncle Scott returned home from Vietnam offered up one of these inexplicable windfalls. Almost without trying, I got her to buy me a box of Count Chocula containing a small brown Frisbee with an image of the Count himself embossed on it. Never in the history of breakfast cereals had there been a prize so sweet.

With nine people living in five bedrooms, space was always at a premium in our house, and when Uncle Scott came to stay, that situation only intensified. Rather than asking the returned hero to sleep on the couch or on a cot in the TV room, my mother gave Scott one of the basement bedrooms normally occupied by my brothers Joe and Steve, which meant they had to move in upstairs with my brother Paul and me. Other things changed as well. For years we had sat down to the evening meal at precisely six o'clock, and woe be unto the boy who failed to return home on time. However, now that Uncle Scott had come to stay with us, dinner would sometimes be put off until seven or even eight o'clock while we waited for him to return from one of his jaunts about town or to wake up from one of the long naps he liked to take most afternoons.

The worst violation of these codes of ours occurred on Easter Sunday. As with the six o'clock dinner hour, the agenda for this holiday had been established long ago. We'd rise early, raid our Easter baskets, hurry to make the ten o'clock Mass at Sacred Heart Cathedral, and then eat a large Easter lunch sometime around noon or one o'clock. But this time, though Paul and I were up at the crack of dawn as usual, we weren't allowed to touch our baskets or eat much of our candy because "Uncle Scott's not up yet." He still wasn't up when we left for Mass at 9:30 that morning or when we returned home at 11:15. This alone was an astonishing fact to behold. Never in my life had I seen an adult sleep so late (both of my parents habitually rose before six), and yet Uncle Scott was just getting started. Noon came and went. One o'clock. Two. By then I was beside myself with anger and frustration. Was Easter itself going to be called off because of one man's inability to get his ass out of bed?

I complained bitterly to my mother, but all she'd say was that we'd eat Easter dinner "when Uncle Scott gets up, not before," adding, in a cruel twist, that no more candy was to be eaten lest we ruin our appetites. I stewed over this injustice in my room, but finally I could take no more and crept down the basement stairs to have a look in Uncle Scott's room. Pushing the door open slowly, I stuck my head inside.

All was quiet except for the sound of Uncle Scott's labored breathing. Pushing the door open farther, I crept into the room on all fours like a soldier negotiating razor wire. I could see everything fine because Uncle Scott had left a reading lamp on above his head. In fact, the lamp shone directly into his ghastly white face. *My God, how can he sleep like that with a hundred-watt bulb shining directly into his eyes?* I wondered.

A moment later, I saw something that to my mind was even more horrifying. Sitting atop a stack of paperbacks next to the bed, filled to the brim with crushed cigarette butts, was my Count Chocula Frisbee. Uncle Scott had turned the treasure upside down and used it as an ashtray.

My mind slowly filled with rage. *What the . . . ? How on . . . ? WHY?!?*

But even as these thoughts reverberated through me, I knew that any desire for retribution was pointless. My mother wouldn't hear a word against "poor Scott." The most I could accomplish in the way of revenge would be to ruin the man's afternoon nap, and so, on the way out of there, I shoved a Jethro Tull tape into my brother Joe's 8-track and turned the thing on full blast.

The image of the desecrated Frisbee was the first thing that came to mind when my mother informed me that we were on a mission to "check on" Uncle Scott.

"Do you even know where he lives?" I asked.

"It's somewhere around here," she answered. "Quit worrying and help me look. Maybe you'll spot him."

We rolled down street after street of dilapidated houses. After thirty minutes of what seemed like aimless searching, my mother began to stop people on the street to ask if they knew where Uncle Scott was staying. Most of the people she asked expressed surprise at our stated mission. I remember in particular a skinny black man with an unkempt Afro who leaned into the window on my side of the car and asked, in a wine-coated voice, "Who the hell are *y'all* looking for *down here?*"

Just the way he said the words *y'all* and *down here* was enough to make my blood run cold, but my mother, for her part, appeared un-fazed. "Scott McDonald," she answered calmly. "He's about your age and build, brown hair and green eyes. The last time I talked to him, he said he was staying with friends somewhere near here."

The man laughed. "Friends, huh? That's a good one. I'm sorry, lady, but I don't think I can help you."

"Well, thank you all the same," my mother said.

"You're welcome," the man said, shaking his head.

A former cheerleader and homecoming queen, my mother was a tall, angular woman with high cheekbones and large, expressive eyes. Even if I'd been incapable of perceiving her beauty, I still would've known all about it, because throughout my childhood, other people, particularly my mother's friends, were forever pointing it out to me. *Seven kids and a waist like a ballerina! How does your mother do it? Do you know who your mom reminds me of? Susan Sarandon, that's who!* Now here she was on a street without a name asking favors of the sort of people she never came into contact with in the usual run of her life. Evidently no part of this troubled her, but the same could not be said for me. Try as I might to avoid it, I couldn't help but imagine terrible things happening to both of us, and of course I blamed Uncle Scott for all of it. Didn't he have a phone she could call to "check up" on him? What the hell was wrong with him anyway? Why couldn't he be counted on the way virtually all of the men I'd grown up around could be?

Then a man, pretty much a carbon copy of the first guy, except that this man was white, approached our car and told us he would take us to Uncle Scott.

"Oh, thanks so much," my mother said.

I expected the man to climb into the car with us, but to my sur-prise he led us down the street on foot, walking in front of our red Impala like Daniel Boone leading a wagon train of pioneers into the wilds of Kentucky. At the end of a narrow street of broken asphalt, we came upon an oblong clapboard house that looked more like a cow shed or an army barracks than an actual house. The house had no number or mailbox, and all of the windows had been covered from the inside with blankets and cardboard.

"This is the place," the skinny man said, leaning in my window. "I'd go up there and get him for you, but there's people in there who don't like me."

"I understand," my mother said. "You've been very helpful as it is."

Here the man paused significantly. "You wouldn't happen to, you know, have a dollar or two for a hungry vet, would you?"

"Sorry, of course," my mother said, digging in her purse.

"Keep the money low," the man said, his hand coming though the car window to snatch up the five-dollar bill she offered. "People are watching." Then he was gone, limping up the street in the direction from which we'd just come.

I wanted to say to my mother that she'd overpaid the man, that he'd almost certainly given us bogus information, that we should leave now while we were still alive, but I could get none of this out before she abandoned me there with orders to "keep the windows rolled up and the doors locked" while she was gone. I can still see her walking up that broken sidewalk and pounding on the door of that ramshackle building. Everything about her, from the peach-colored dress she wore to the way her purse hung from her slender arm, cried out that she had no business stepping foot in that neighborhood, let alone pounding on doors and making demands of strangers. I wanted to roll down that window and shout for her to come back at once. I wanted to say to her, *What about me, Mom? Don't you understand that I'm big enough to sense the danger you're in and yet not nearly big enough to do anything to protect you? Am I really supposed to just sit here in this locked car and hope for the best? How long am I supposed to wait? A minute? Five minutes? An hour?*

Then the door to the house opened and a shirtless man with tattoos up and down his arms appeared. The two of them exchanged a series of frantic words and gestures, then the door shut again and my mother resumed her pounding. A few seconds later, a second man opened the door and yelled something at my mother, whereupon she put both hands on her hips (a gesture I knew well) and yelled right back at him. Finally the door opened wider and Uncle Scott appeared. I recognized him despite the fact that he looked nothing like the shorthaired, clean-shaven soldier I remembered from the year before. Apparently that version of Uncle Scott was gone forever, replaced by a version with long, bushy hair and a three- or four-day growth of beard. (I remember thinking, *My God, he looks like Shaggy on* Scooby-Doo.) They talked a minute on the doorstep, then Uncle Scott disappeared back into the house, and my mother walked back to the car and got in.

"Who are those people?" I asked as soon as she shut her door.

"I don't know," she answered.

"Where's Uncle Scott? Is he coming?"

"Yes."

"Are we going to leave soon?"

"Yes! Now stop asking so many questions."

Her hands shook as she lit a cigarette and blew the smoke out the window.

A few minutes later, Uncle Scott came out of the house in sandals and a green army jacket and got into the front seat of the car with us.

"Hey, Champ," he said as his shoulder bumped into mine.

"Hey," I said, moving over.

His right hand was covered in a dirty white bandage, but I didn't ask about that. I was waiting for one thing and one thing only, and that was to get the hell out of there.

We went to a nondescript diner with a long buffet where old people piled their plates high with fruit and cottage cheese. Since I'd been holding out hope for McDonald's—A&W at the very least—this choice of restaurant was a great disappointment to me. When my mother, scanning the menu, asked what looked good to me, I shrugged and said I didn't care. I think I ordered a hot dog, while Uncle Scott ordered meat loaf and coffee.

After the waitress left with our orders, Uncle Scott laughed and shook his head in that pathetic, hangdog way he had, as if the world we lived in was nothing but an elaborate joke and his part in the cosmic drama was not to take any of it too seriously.

"How have you been doing?" my mother asked him. "Are you working?"

"I was until this happened," he answered, holding up his bandaged right hand. As my mother and I watched, he unwound the dirty bandage to reveal a pinky finger that was swollen to twice its usual size with a series of ghastly black stitches running up one side.

"Oh, Scott," my mother said. "Have you seen a doctor?"

"Sure. How do you think I got the stitches?"

"I mean lately," my mother said. "It looks infected."

"Oh, it's all right," Uncle Scott said, rewinding the bandage around the injured hand and dropping it into his lap again.

Our food arrived, and I tore into mine, polishing it off in a matter of minutes along with two large glasses of root beer. For his part, Uncle Scott just pushed his meatloaf around the gravy on his plate. He took a few bites of mashed potatoes, then called the waitress back and got a refill on his coffee.

"The whole time I was in the army, it was nothing but *meat loaf, meat loaf, meat loaf,*" he laughed. "You'd think that in a place like Vietnam they'd serve you *rice* or something, but you'd be wrong about that. Uncle Sam likes his meat loaf, mashed potatoes, and gravy." Here he looked directly at me, as though noticing me for the first time. "You had to see the doctor, huh? What about?"

"Something to do with my brain," I answered. "They hooked me up to San Francisco, but we won't get the results for a while."

This brought another of his trademark laughs. "Your *brain,* huh? Well, don't listen to them. What the hell do doctors know about what goes on in our *brains?*"

"If you're not working," my mother interjected, "then what are you doing?"

"Oh, you know. This and that. I get by all right."

"It doesn't look like it to me, Scott. You don't look *well*."

He shrugged the comment off and, reaching across the table, shook one of my mother's cigarettes out of its package. "You mind?"

"No," she answered. "Go right ahead."

I could feel the tension rising between them, and I tried to diffuse it by asking questions.

"Uncle Scott, how long were you in Vietnam?"

"Eleven months and fourteen days."

"What was your job?"

"I was a grunt, son, the lowest of the low."

"Did you shoot anyone?"

"Robby!" my mother said.

"It's all right," Uncle Scott laughed from behind a wall of smoke. Turning to me, he added, very matter-of-factly, "Your Uncle Randy was in a helicopter gunship. I'm pretty sure he shot a lot of people. But I was just a grunt. I got shot *at* some, but I never returned the favor. Truth is, I went through the whole war without even firing my weapon at anything more than shadows."

I nodded, sorely disappointed by this confession.

"I did get really scared once, though. Do you want to hear about it?"

"Sure."

"Scott," my mother began.

"Oh, stop worrying," Uncle Scott responded. "I won't say anything to *damage* the kid or anything."

He told a strange story about an unsettling couple of hours he'd spent on guard duty while the rest of his unit slept nearby.

"We were camped on the edge of a clearing in the jungle, some godforsaken place we'd humped to that day, and it was my job to watch the clearing and report on any, quote unquote, suspicious activity." Dragging from his cigarette, he used his clawlike fingers to make quote marks in the air. "But the thing is, when you're that scared, *everything* is suspicious. The wind is suspicious. The moon and the clouds moving across the moon are suspicious. The sounds of the jungle at night—insects buzzing around, monkeys screaming—hell, it's *all* suspicious. After a while, your eyes get to playing tricks on you. You begin to believe you can see things that may or may not be there. And what I saw, late that night, just as sure as I'm sitting here, was a gook coming out of the trees and beginning to crawl toward us across the clearing."

I could feel my mother flinch at the word *gook*, but I was enthralled.

"Really?" I asked. "What did you do?"

"What did I do?" Scott repeated, as though posing the question to himself for the first time. "Well, I'll tell you what I didn't do. I didn't shoot off a flare, or go wake someone up and ask for help, or any of the other things I probably should've done. I still don't know why. I guess I was just too goddamn scared."

"Scott," my mother said again, but he held up his hand, stopping her.

"I just kept sitting there, squinting my eyes in the dark, praying to God they were playing some kind of trick on me. I'm telling you, it was *terrible*, the worst night of my entire life by a long shot. I wanted to yell out to the guy in the clearing, *Hey, you stupid goddamn gook, can't you see I've got a gun over here and I'm going to have to put a bullet in your brain if you get any closer?* I kept imagining myself squeezing the trigger of that gun. *Bam bam bam bam*—right through his brain. But the more I imagined it, the more scared I got."

"Then what happened?"

"Yes, finish your story," my mother said.

"I will, but you're not going to like it," Uncle Scott said, crushing his cigarette in the ashtray and taking another one from my mother's pack. "Morning happened. The sun came up, and by the light of day I saw very clearly that the gook I'd been so worried about all night long was a fucking water buffalo."

"You're kidding," I said.

"No, I'm not."

"A water buffalo?"

"Yeah, *hee hee hee*, a fucking water buffalo!"

Again, I felt my mother flinch.

"And that's it?" I asked. "That's the whole story?"

"That's it," Scott said, shaking his head. "Hey, I *told you* you wouldn't like it."

"Oh, Scott," my mother said, reaching for a cigarette herself now.

"What can I say? The human brain's a very kooky thing. Just ask Champ here, *hee hee hee.*"

For my part I just sat there, massively disappointed, watching without comprehension as tears rolled down my mother's face, streaking in her makeup.

"Who wants dessert?" she asked after a while, wiping at her eyes with a napkin.

"I do!"

"None for me," Uncle Scott said.

Later, as I was finishing off an ice cream sundae, she asked if maybe Uncle Scott would like to go bowling with us. It was a very strange request, I thought. We were not exactly a bowling family. Never had been.

"Well, I would," Scott said, holding up his bandaged right hand with its hideous pinky finger, "but I don't think I'd be *able to*, you know?" And here again, he laughed his hideous laugh.

After my mother paid the check, we drove back to the neighborhood where we'd found Uncle Scott earlier that day.

"Anywhere along here is fine," he said, opening the door before my mother had even brought the car to a halt. Did she offer him money? She must have. And he must have taken it, too.

"Take care of yourself," I remember her calling after him as he climbed out of the Impala. "Call me if you need anything."

I don't remember him saying anything in return.

As soon as we were back on the road to Dodge City, my mother crushed the pack of cigarettes she'd shared with Uncle Scott and threw it out the window.

"Why'd you do that?" I asked, shocked by this act of littering.

"I made a promise to God," she said without looking at me. "If it

turned out there was nothing wrong with you, I'd quit smoking forever. So that's it. I'm finished."

"But we haven't gotten the results back," I reminded her.

"A promise is a promise," she answered. "I'm finished with them.
I'll never smoke another cigarette as long as I live."

She didn't, either.

A week or two after this, we got a letter from the hospital in Wichita. The EEG had turned up nothing—no brain tumor, no sign of epi-
lepsy or anything else that might have brought on my "episodes."

"What did I tell you?" my father said at dinner that night. "Just
look at him. Perfectly healthy kid."

"Well, better safe than sorry," my mother said, smiling in a way
that reassured me that everything was about to go back to normal
again.

I was in graduate school in Buffalo, New York, many years later
when my mother called to tell me that Uncle Scott had died of an over-
dose in a Wichita motel room. He was forty-two years old and had
been addicted to one drug or another for the better part of twenty-five
years. Hearing the news, I immediately thought of that trip to Wichita
we'd taken together all those years ago, every last detail of it coming
back to me as clearly as if I were watching it unfold on a movie screen.

"How old was Uncle Scott back then?" I asked.

"I don't know, twenty-two or twenty-three. About the same age
you are now."

I shook a cigarette out of a pack on my kitchen table and stood
looking out the window at a skinny man in an army jacket panhan-
dling passers-by. He was out there most days, but somehow his pres-
ence had never registered the way it did now.

"You know," my mother continued, "it was on that trip to Wichita
that I first understood the choice I had to make. I could try to save
poor Scott, or I could protect you kids from him, but I couldn't do
both. God help me, but it just wasn't going to be possible."

I lit the cigarette and inhaled deeply. Outside, the first snow of
the year had begun to fall. The man in the army jacket moved lazily

up the street. I could barely make out his drab green jacket amid the falling snow.

"Hell of a choice," I said.

"Yes," my mother said, exhaling as though for both of us. "Yes, it was."

—3—
A Fire on the Moon

In the world of build-it-yourself, dirt-track jalopy racing, the National Modified Championships at Hutchinson or, more simply, "The Nationals," were as big as things got, and no one involved in racing in southwest Kansas would have considered missing them. Certainly that was the case for my family that summer of 1974. My father and his brother Harold had been building open-wheeled jalopies—typically 1930s flathead Fords with the fenders removed and a roll cage welded to the frame—and dragging them to various dirt tracks on the southern high plains since the mid-1950s. Then, in May 1974, my family's fanaticism grew even stronger when my brother Alan, just days removed from his high school graduation, began driving a late-model stock car in the weekend races held at Dodge City's McCarty Speedway.

The weekend routine rarely varied. Late Friday night or early Saturday morning, Alan's #17 Chevelle would be loaded onto a flatbed tow truck and delivered to our house so that my brother Paul and I, ages six and nine, could go to work washing and waxing it. This we accomplished with an air of self-importance, lording it over our friends in the neighborhood who, by decree of our father, were not allowed anywhere near the car lest they break something or "fall off the truck and sue us." When the job was done, Alan would emerge from the house with his Bell helmet and Simpson Flame Resistant Nomex® fire suit, followed a few minutes later by a pit crew made up of my brothers Tom, Joe, and Steve, all of them wearing navy blue #17 jumpsuits my mother had embroidered by hand. To a kid of six or nine years old, this was a thrilling sight to behold, on par with watching astronauts stroll across a sun-splashed tarmac on their way to being loaded into a lunar capsule. Not long after they drove off to "secure a good spot in the pits," Paul and I, wearing our own #17 jackets, would accompany our mother to the 5:30 Mass at Sacred Heart Cathedral, where we would be instructed to "say a prayer that your brother doesn't get himself killed tonight."

This I did in an entirely rote manner. In the two or three years I'd been going to the races at McCarty Speedway, I'd seen cars spin out, crash into one another, roll over, and flip high into the air, and always the drivers emerged unscathed from the wreckage. Occasionally an ambulance would arrive on the scene and a driver would be hauled to the local hospital as a precaution, but he'd always be back in action the following weekend. Where was the risk in that?

After Mass let out at 6:30, my mother would steer the family's Buick Skylark into a long line of pickups and cars streaming from Wyatt Earp Boulevard to the track in Wright Park. The atmosphere in this procession of cars was festive bordering on raucous. Men and teenage boys, some of them shirtless and tattooed, yelled and threw beer cans at each other from the backs of pickups. Whenever a streetlight switched from red to green, the car at the front of the line would peel out, and one by one the cars just behind would follow suit, until the air on the street was filled with the smell of burning rubber. Meanwhile, fans of the different drivers would taunt each other from open windows ("Your boy's gonna finish *dead last*. Just you wait!"), while fans of a different sort drunkenly reveled in the prospect of disaster ("Here's hoping we see some big wrecks tonight!"). According to our mother, we were "better than that," "cut from a different bolt of cloth." However, that did not make us any less competitive, and if anyone dared to yell an insult about the #17 car, you can bet that Paul and I were quick to answer in kind. "Oh, yeah? Well, get ready to eat some dust, buddy!"

Once a parking place had been secured in the buffalo grass lining the Arkansas River, another line awaited us at the gate to the concrete grandstands, in the belly of which men with cigarettes hanging from their lips rented out cushioned seatbacks and sold T-shirts embla-

zoned with the name and number of this or that driver—#98 Rod
Keller, #15 J. D. Martin, #77 Jack Petty, #11 Jim Harkness. Next came
the crush of humanity lining up before the hotdog and Coke stands,
past which our mother always dragged us unrelentingly, her hands
locked around our wrists in a death grip. "Come *on*, boys. You've already eaten, for goodness' sake!"

By the time we got into our seats halfway up the grandstand, the
water truck would be wetting down the track and a motley crew of
race cars, both late-model stocks and open-wheeled supermodifieds,
would be busy packing down the ⅜-mile clay oval. The noise made
by these machines was as yet a dull roar, a mere foreboding compared
to what lay ahead when the actual races started. It was still possible
to shout a message to the person sitting next to you and be heard,
maybe even understood. After the heat races started, that would no
longer be the case. By then the steady, ear-splitting roar of the engines,
along with the dust rising up from the track and the mud flying from
the cars' tires as they slid through the turns, would produce a state of
deaf-muteness/tunnel vision among all in attendance. To communi-
cate required shoving the person next to you to get his or her attention
and following that up with a kind of frantic, improvised sign language.
C-A-N EYE G-O 2 T-H-E RESTROOOOOOOM??? And the longer the race
went on, the deeper this trancelike state became, until finally it was so
deep and intense as to be physically painful. Everywhere in the stands,
people would cup their hands over their ears and squint, or in some
cases close their eyes, against the rising dust. Meanwhile, an overpow-
ering, scorched smell—a mixture of cascading dirt, engine exhaust,
burning rubber, and cigarette smoke—pervaded the air. Once a race
had reached this state of fever pitch, only two things could bring it to
a halt: a checkered flag, signifying completion of the allotted number
of laps, or else a yellow or black flag, signifying a wreck or some other
danger on the track.

All this was nothing, however, compared with what happened
whenever one of Alan's races came up, for on these occasions my
mother's anxiety would ramp up to its highest gear. As a pack of cars

took to the track and the #17 Chevelle was spotted among them, she'd reach out and involuntarily take hold of whichever of my knees was closest to her. Then as the green flag dropped, and Alan began to make his way to the front of the pack, bumping and grinding and trading paint, sliding into the banked corners side by side with whatever car he was trying to pass, then diving low and accelerating into the long front- or backstretch, the grip she'd taken on my knee or thigh would increase exponentially. The closer to real or theoretical danger Alan came, the harder she gripped my leg. If he happened to spin out or crash into another car, she'd raise both of her hands up to her face and then, just as quickly, slam them back down, reestablishing her death grip. The next morning I'd wake to find a series of bluish-purple bruises running up and down my leg. This behavior of my mother's annoyed and embarrassed me, but on another level I understood and even admired it. It meant that she was even more deeply immersed in the racing experience than I was. After a time, I came to accept the bruises she inflicted on me as the emblem of what racing had come to mean to her, if not yet to me—an impossibly loud marathon of witnessed and/or experienced terror.

To me and my brother Paul, the best part of a night of racing occurred at the end, after the feature race was over and fans began to leave the stands accompanied by race promoter Jack Merrick's familiar voice: "Thank you and we'll see you again next week." That's when a big gate at the bottom of the grandstands swung open, and diehard fans like us were allowed to spill out onto the track. Paul and I were always among the first kids out of the gate. Our goal was to scour the track for as many plastic tear-away visor guards as we could collect. All night long, as their faces were assaulted with mud and dust, drivers had been tearing these strips of plastic from their helmet visors and tossing them out of their car windows. Now a reverse process was under way, as kids raced each other around the banked oval in a bid to be declared the unofficial winner of our own "trophy dash." What a surreal experience it was to be out there on the hard-packed, high-banked, floodlit clay, the dust and engine exhaust from the A Feature still floating in the air like a fog. Looking up at the moon so high in the night sky, I'd sometimes pretend that that's where *we* were and that the moon was, by process of substitution, an impossibly small Planet Earth.

Once we'd had our fill of the track, Paul and I would venture into the pits proper, where drivers and pit crew members leaned against or sat on the hoods of their battered cars, smoking cigarettes and sucking down cans of Coors. Although it was the 1970s and young drivers like my brother often had shoulder-length hair, the older drivers sported a look straight out of the 1950s. These were men of my father's generation. They slicked their hair straight back from their foreheads in a style known as a DA or "duck's ass," and if they wore a fire suit at all (many didn't), they'd step out of it as soon as their last race was over, preferring to receive the public in rolled-at-the-ankle jeans and a white T-shirt with a pack of unfiltered Camels rolled into one of the sleeves. Whoever had won the Trophy Dash that night—invariably it was one of these men—would have the foot-high prize prominently displayed on the hood or roof of his car. I remember one such car with particular vividness. It was the #77 Mustang driven by a man from Wichita named Jack Petty. Everything about the car, from its flaming orange-and-yellow paint job to the way Petty's name was etched above the door in two-tone cursive lettering, spoke to me. It said "coolness" and "outlaw" and "raw speed." Above all, it said "danger."

I couldn't help but compare all this to the effect produced by my brother's fire-engine red #17 Chevelle, every detail of which I was intimately familiar with from having washed and waxed it so many times. Whereas the #77 Mustang was driven from the left like a street-legal car, allowing Petty to wave to the crowd or hold a checkered flag out his window as he took a victory lap, Alan's car had been reconfigured by my father (no doubt at my mother's insistence) so that it was driven from the *middle*, like a sprint car or a supermodified. That is to say, both the driver's seat and the steering wheel had been moved so that they sat atop the automatic transmission, a configuration that allowed Alan to steer the car through the entirety of a race without ever taking his hands from the wheel. But this was not the only safety feature. There was the bright red fire extinguisher strapped to the inside of the car's extensive roll cage and, just behind Alan, in the car's reinforced trunk area, the high-tech fuel cell with its plastic bladder stuffed with foam to keep gas from leaking, sloshing around in the tank, or exploding in the event of a crash or rollover. All of this was impressive, to be sure, but it was also vaguely embarrassing, maybe even a little shameful. I used to complain about it to my older brothers whenever Alan and my father weren't around. "Who drives a stock car from the *middle* instead of the side? Definitely *not cool.*"

"You only think that because you've never seen a really bad pile-up," my brother Tom replied with a shrug. "Once you've seen one of those, you'll change your tune in a hurry."

"Maybe," I said doubtfully.

As an eighteen-year-old racing men often twice his age, Alan tended to be a cautious driver who took what a race gave him and did not test the limits of what he or his car could do the way some drivers did. Still he won a lot of heat races that summer. He even won a semifinal or two. And usually he finished near the front of the A Feature. These were sizable accomplishments, particularly for a driver as young as he was. However, in my even younger eyes, all of this success was beside the point. To hell with heat races and the long, overly loud feature. The race I wanted to see Alan win was the Trophy Dash—that quick, four or five-lap sprint in the middle of the evening's races that determined which driver got to kiss the trophy girl while a photographer from the Dodge City *Daily Globe* snapped his picture. How I longed to run into the pits, my ears ringing, to find that night's hardware sitting proudly atop the red hood of the #17 Chevelle. But it never happened.

Even so, I admired my brother greatly. Two or three times a week, while he and my father were away at the shop "slaving over that car," as my mother always put it, I would sneak into Alan's room in the basement of our house and put on his fire suit, gloves, and full-face helmet, then stand looking at myself in the room's full-length mirror. The suit, a secondhand Simpson, was white with royal blue stripes running down the arms and legs. (One of these stripes, I think it was on the left side, had been burned off the suit before Alan bought it, causing my mother to sew a new one in its place.) Of course, the suit was too big for me—the arms and legs were a foot or more too long, the gloves always threatening to fall off my hands. However, I saw no comedy in this. Or, if I did, I gave it only the slightest notice. What I saw when I looked in that mirror was an older, taller version of myself climbing out of Jack Petty's orange-and-yellow #77 Mustang to claim yet another prize from a stunningly beautiful trophy girl. I imagined the scenario so many times that I had both sides of the postrace interview memorized.

Q. You won again! How do you do it?
A. Well, I only know one way to race—pedal to the metal.
Q. Aren't you afraid of crashing or rolling your car?
A. Nah. That's what tow trucks are for—to pick up the pieces.
Q. What about the other cars and drivers? Do you have anything to say to them?
A. As a matter of fact, I do. Go fast or get the hell out of the way.

At the end of the interview, I'd take an imaginary comb from my pocket and drag it through an improvised duck's ass, precisely the way I'd seen my favorite drivers do in the moment before the photographer's flashbulb exploded in their smiling faces.

By the end of that summer, Alan had racked up enough points at McCarty Speedway to claim Rookie of the Year honors in the late-model stock division. This was quite an accomplishment, and it came with a trophy and a notice in the *Daily Globe* (albeit, sadly, with no kiss from a trophy girl). Despite this success, however, my father and mother agreed that Alan was still too young and inexperienced to race in that year's season-ending Nationals in Hutchinson, as Jack Petty and a hundred other drivers would do. As a consolation of sorts, he'd be allowed to watch the race from turn one in the pits, while the rest of the family, including my parents and four of my brothers, sat high in the grandstands along with ten thousand other dirt track race fans.

The Sunday of the 1974 Nationals turned out to be a hot, dry day "without a whisper of breeze," as one of the drivers later said. My family made the two-hour trip from Dodge City to Hutchinson in the cool morning hours, arriving at the State Fairgrounds long before the first race began. In my mind, this meant that we'd have time to take a stroll down the Midway, maybe even go for a ride on the Zipper, an amusement park ride then at the height of its fame. But I was wrong about all that. "The Fair's not until September," my father reminded me. "There's a race then, too, but it's nowhere near as big as the one we're going to."

With all hope for a ride on the Zipper lost, I had nothing to look forward to except the races themselves, which I imagined to be identical to those held in Dodge City. After all, both races were put on by the same promoter, big-voiced Jack Merrick. But it turned out I was wrong about that, too. While the grandstands at McCarty Speedway held perhaps two thousand spectators, the stands at the Fairgrounds held more than five times that number, and that was not counting the fans who climbed onto the roof or stood with their fingers poking through the fence at the edge of the track. I marveled at all of this as we made our way to our seats, halfway up the grandstands and just in front of the flagman's tower.

By the time the first heat race was set to begin, the temperature on the track was somewhere north of 100 degrees, and it wasn't much cooler where we sat. Several drivers had ditched their gloves, and some had ditched their fire suits as well, choosing to drive in T-shirts instead. Everywhere in the stands, people fanned themselves with race programs or wrapped wet kerchiefs around their necks. Rumor had it that more than 110 cars had participated in qualifying the day before. How many of these would survive the heat races and end up in the thirty-lap late model feature or the even bigger fifty-lap supermodified feature was anyone's guess.

"It's gonna be crazy no matter what," my brother Steve predicted. "Fifty cars in a feature! Holy cow!"

"Just say a prayer no one gets hurt," my mother said.

I looked at Steve, and we both laughed. This was just Mom being Mom. Evidently there was something wrong with her that made her say these crazy things all the time. Who knew what it was?

After the national anthem was sung, the first heat races got under way. As usual, these were a carnival of noise and rising dust. I covered my ears with my hands and watched to see how my favorite drivers would do. I saw that #98 Rod Keller finished near the front in one of the heat races, as did #15 J. D. Martin in another. In the final heat for stock cars, #77 Jack Petty of Wichita took first, while two Dodge City drivers, #8 Don Kreie and #12 Tim Wheaton, finished not far behind him. This was a thrilling result, but by the end of the stock car heats, my interest had begun to wane. I knew few of the cars in the modified class beyond #11 Jim Harkness of Ness City. Instead of watching the races, I began to campaign for a trip to the concessions stand. And for once my mother agreed to let me go, provided a couple of my older brothers went along. We spent the next several races in the shade of the grandstands, sucking down Cokes and gawking at the trophies that would be given to the winners of the two features.

We made it back to our seats in time for the late model feature. It was an exciting race. Jack Petty started on the pole, and he held that lead for seventeen laps before being passed by Dodge City's Don Kreie. Then Petty caught Kreie on the very next lap and managed to hold the lead for another five laps until he and Kreie traded paint in one of the corners and Petty's car blew a rear tire, falling all the way to last place. By then, the noise of the race was almost unbearable, and the dust rising up from the track was so thick it was hard to see who was leading or even which car was which. To keep from choking, I pulled the collar of my T-shirt over my mouth and nose. After a few laps, I pulled the shirt up over my eyes as well. I didn't even see Kreie take the checkered flag but only heard about it when Jack Merrick announced the winner over the PA system.

There was one more race to go—the massive fifty-lap feature that would determine the Nationals champion in the open-wheeled super-modified division. As the dust settled, race fans speculated on who would take home the trophy. Would it be #11 Jim Harkness of Ness City, #86 Jon Johnson of Utica, #4 Grady Wade of Wichita? But there was even more discussion of the "dry-slick" condition of the track and how hot it was.

"What are they gonna do about the dirt?" my mother asked. "The drivers can hardly see in front of themselves! It's like the Dust Bowl out there!"

"I don't know, but I'm sure they'll get it figured out," my father said, sounding none too sure about this.

A water truck headed onto the track and began to wet down the lowest part of the banked oval. But after only a couple of laps, the truck headed back into the pits, and Merrick called for the drivers to take to the track for the main event.

"That's it?" my mother asked. "That's all the water they're putting on the track? Is that gonna be enough, Bill?"

"I guess it'll have to be," my father said ominously.

I remember thinking how odd it was to have him in the stands with us. It should have made me feel safer and more confident, but something like the reverse was true. With him there, my mother kept none of her concerns to herself. It was too hot. The track was too dry. There were too many cars. I was almost glad when the noise of the cars coming onto the track finally got to be loud enough that she had to quit fretting and watch the race like the rest of us.

More than forty cars were lined up two abreast on the flat half-mile oval. They stretched from the pole position just underneath the flagman's stand all the way back into turn four. Forty cars were at least fifteen more than I had ever seen on one track before. The cars were a motley crew. Some were new and sleek-looking—something like a contemporary sprint car but without the massive wing mounted to the roof. Others looked like the jalopies my father and his brother Harold used to make out of Model A Fords in the 1950s. One of these cars, painted in primer with a number made out of duct tape, had an orange, slow-moving-vehicle triangle mounted above its rear bumper. In some cases, the drivers of these cars lacked full-face helmets, and several were without gloves, having sworn these off earlier in the day when they had trouble tearing away dirt-covered visor guards.

An ominous dust cloud began to form even before the pace lap was complete. By the time the race leaders had taken the green flag, the cloud was so thick that visibility farther back in the pack couldn't have been more than twenty or thirty feet. It was scary how quickly the cloud had grown and how loud the cars were. It was more like what you might expect from the middle or the end of a feature, not the beginning. As I pulled my shirt up to my nose, I could feel the familiar trance / tunnel vision coming over me.

Then it happened. As Harkness and the other leaders completed their first lap, a hard-charging car farther back in the pack came upon one of the slower cars and accidentally ran up over its exposed rear tire. Instantly the faster car was launched high into the air. A collective gasp went up in the grandstands as the car flipped end over end before landing hard at the entrance to turn one. Its front axle flew off and began rolling in the direction of the flagman's tower, and I felt my mother's hand grabbing at my leg.

"Oh God, no! Oh God, *no!*"

But there was nothing anyone could do to stop what was about to happen. We just sat there as car after car, blinded by the dust, drove straight into the growing pile-up. Some hit the pile head on. Others, catching a glimpse of the wreck, hit the brakes at the last second and slid into the pile sideways. After watching five or six cars hit the pile, I turned and looked at the cars coming out of turn four. They had no idea what lay ahead. The dust was too thick. One after another, they, too, joined the smash-up.

Then a fuel tank on one of the cars exploded and caught fire, sending a thirty-foot tower of flames and billowing black smoke skyward. Drivers began to spill out of the wrecked cars willy-nilly, as crewmen from the pits ran forward with fire extinguishers in a vain attempt to keep the fire from spreading. It was a good idea, but it did nothing. One car after another was engulfed in flames.

My mother tried to cover my eyes with her hands, but I broke away from her. I saw one of the drivers climb out of the roof of his burning car, his arms held out to his sides in a Christ-like pose. His entire body was on fire. He stood there a long moment, as though trying to decide what to do, then leaped from the burning wreck in the direction of the infield, where two men grabbed him by his arms and dragged him into the grass. Another driver, his body charred and smoking, lay in the middle of the track, not fifty yards from where I sat. I squeezed my eyes shut, only to open them again a few seconds later. I kept doing this, over and over.

The fire was so intense I could feel it on my face, arms, and the front of my legs. I could feel it in my hair. I remember thinking, *It's an inferno, like that blimp, the Hindenburg. It's gonna burn and burn until everyone is dead and nothing is left but ashes.*

More men ran forward from the pits with fire extinguishers, but their efforts were like throwing a bucket of water into a bonfire. Jack Merrick came on the PA to say that someone should call the fire department. But no trucks arrived, and the fire burned on, one explosion following another, until finally all thirteen cars involved in the wreck were consumed.

Four or five minutes into the disaster, Merrick announced that a fire engine had arrived at the south gate of the track. But it turned out the gate was locked, no one knew who had the key, and the firemen had to drive all the way around the track to find an open gate, and another five minutes passed before water was finally brought to bear on the flames. Meanwhile, a couple of ambulances arrived to carry away the drivers who had been burned. Even then, cars that had been dragged away from the pile continued to burst into flames. Each time it happened, the crowd would flinch and my mother would call out, "Oh God, oh God, *no!*" Ten minutes after the flip that caused the wreck, several smaller fires were still going, while the whole area before turn one, where the pile-up had occurred, was reduced to a charred ruin.

"Please, people, move back away from the fence," Merrick called out over the PA. "Move away from the infield, and let the firemen do their work."

By now it was clear that the race could never continue, and the crowd of thousands began to flow toward the exits.

"Let's go," my father said.

"What about Alan?" my mother asked.

"He knows where we parked. Come on."

As we joined the exodus, Jack Merrick came on the PA and said in a dazed voice, "Thank you very much, and we'll see you next year."

It was the sort of thing he always said after a race was over, and usually it was received without comment as mere background noise. Not this time.

"He's telling us *thank you?*" someone near us said loudly. "To *hell* with that!" Other voices soon joined in. "Too many cars. No fire trucks. Should've never run the last race. Should've put more water on that track."

We found Alan slumped against the Buick in the grass parking lot. He looked stunned. "Are you all right?" my mother asked. "The wreck must have happened right in front of you."

"It did," Alan said.

But when we asked him what he had seen, he just shook his head and climbed into the very back of the car, refusing to talk about it. He would race a couple more years at our local track in Dodge City, then our father sold his parts business to go back into farming and ranching, and Alan quit racing soon after that. When I asked him how he could abandon something that had loomed so large in his life, he just shrugged and said, "I don't know. Just got to be too expensive, I guess."

We joined a long line of cars making their way from the track. On the radio it was announced that two of the drivers who had been badly burned in the crash, Jerry Soderberg of Dodge City and Jack Petty of Wichita, had been airlifted to the University of Kansas burn center. Another driver, Aaron Madden of Tulsa, was in a trauma unit in Hutchinson.

"That can't be right," I said. "Jack Petty drives a stock car."

"A lot of these guys drive both, particularly at Nationals," my father said in a low voice. "Jack might have done that. You never know."

Newspaper accounts of the fire would confirm my father's suspicion. It was indeed Jack Petty who stood like a burning cross atop his car before making a dramatic leap into the infield. Like all of the drivers, he survived the fire—and in his case even returned to racing. I can recall being at McCarthy Speedway in 1975 or 1976, the last years my brother raced, and seeing Petty circle the track with a checkered flag in his gloved hand. However, I don't recall running into the pits after the race was over in an attempt to get his autograph, and driving home from Hutchinson the night of the fire, I refused to believe he'd even been involved.

Meanwhile, the voices on the radio continued to describe the crash and its aftermath. On and on they droned, repeating the same facts over and over again until finally my mother reached forward and angrily switched the radio off.

"I'm sorry," she said, "but if I have to listen to those idiots for another second, I think I'll go insane."

Nobody objected. We drove the rest of the way home in silence.

—4—

Of Cattle, Bush Hogs, and Men

My long apprenticeship in the cowman's world began in the bicentennial summer of 1976, when my father, who'd just given up the auto parts business to plunge headlong into high-stakes farming and ranching, put me in charge of a bottle calf operation that he and my older brothers had set up behind the round-top shed on our farm eight miles west of Dodge City. I was twelve, and the plan was simple. Every time a cow at the feedlot down the road from the farm unexpectedly dropped a calf, we'd pull a little stock trailer over there and retrieve the orphan. Feedlot cattle, as a rule, are only weeks or months away from the slaughterhouse door. They had no time to raise a calf. If the orphans we brought home in the trailer were to live at all, it would be up to me and bottles of milk replacer to make it happen.

That summer, as the nation celebrated its two hundredth birthday and Bruce Jenner and Nadia Comăneci racked up gold in Montreal, I was busy learning the ins and outs of mothering calves. The trick was to get the calf out of the muck of the feedlot as soon as possible, and then to make sure it got plenty of colostrum (which we bought frozen from a nearby dairy) in the first forty-eight hours of its life. For several weeks after that, until it learned to drink from a bucket, the animal had to be bottle-fed twice a day, the long pink nipple of the plastic quart bottle approximating the size and shape of its mother's udder. At any time in this process, the calf could be laid low with a case of scours, pink eye, or BVD (bovine respiratory disease), in which case it usually died and its body had to be buried behind the round-top. The calves that lived soon graduated to starter feed and finally to hay and grass. In the space of six or seven months, they had been brought

from the brink of death into a stable and secure adolescence in one of
our far-flung pastures.

I remember one of these calves with particular clarity. My younger
brother Paul and I called him "Big Ears" because, although he had the
typical gangly calf body, his ears looked like they'd been transplanted
from a donkey or mule. Often when we were called to the feedlot to
pick up a calf, we'd find it waiting for us in a dry lot or a pen with straw
or sawdust spread across the floor. Not so with Big Ears. He was mired
up to his neck in the muck of the pen where he'd been born, no part of
him visible except for his head and those ridiculous ears. To get him
out, we had to tie a rope around his neck and pull as if the Devil himself were on the other end. Once we got him out of the muck, he lay
on his side panting and coughing, his nose covered with white snot.

"I don't like the sound of that cough," my older brother Joe offered.
"He's a goner for sure."

"We'll see," my father said. "Load him into the trailer, and let's get
to going."

For the first few days after we brought him home, Big Ears wouldn't
drink colostrum or milk replacer. All he did was stand in the corner
of the pen looking off in the direction of the feedlot, his sides heaving.
Meanwhile, several of his pen mates died and were buried. I was sure
that's where Big Ears was headed, too.

But a few days later I brought a bucket of milk replacer into the
pen for another calf, and here came Big Ears, shouldering the other
calf out of the way and draining the bucket in a series of loud, lip-
smacking sucks. Afterwards, he licked his nose clean with a tongue
that rivaled his ears in sheer size.

"Big Ears!" I shouted. "You decided to live!"

And so he had. By the end of that summer he'd joined the older
calves in a nearby pasture, disappearing among them like a sailor
melting into the scene of a crowded port.

⌐⌐

This, I later came to understand, was one of the most dicey and dangerous periods in my father's life. He was forty-three years old and had just abandoned a successful career in the salvage business to return to a life of farming and ranching, a dream he'd carried around with him for at least fifteen years if not longer. (Sometime later, when my mother quietly went back to a career in banking after twenty years and seven children, it occurred to me that women deal with these changes in a way that men know nothing about.) As a result of this huge change in the life of our family, there was a natural division among my six brothers and me according to what kind of forced labor you did in your youth. My oldest brother, Dave, still had the spartan time before our dad quit farming etched into his memory, and, like a convict who had managed to get over the wall, he wasn't about to go back. Meanwhile, my brothers Alan and Tom were so far gone into the grease-monkey world of race cars and motorcycles that they had experienced working for our dad at his salvage business that it was doubtful they would ever be reclaimed. Thus it fell to those of us in the middle of the family, particularly my older brother Joe and me, to follow the old man into the quicksand of high-risk irrigation agriculture.

From the beginning, our dad ran a few head of cattle. He had a few hundred acres of grass here and there, not to mention winter wheat and milo stalks, both of which did better if cattle were rotated on and off at the right time. For a few summers he took on some dairy cows and got paid a set amount for every pound they gained. To get any bigger than that was to talk in terms of a cattle *venture,* the sort of thing that could buy you a new combine if everything went right and break you if the market headed south or if some weather- or illness-related disaster occurred.

In my second summer on the farm, I had a look at one of these cattle ventures up close. A cattle buyer I'll call John Gable had bought a herd of two hundred or so yearling steers and left them with us to feed. It was another one of those per-pound deals, with us handling all of the day-to-day responsibilities and Mr. Gable assuming all of the risk. I remember the day the cattle arrived. Mr. Gable sat in the cab of his long black Lincoln Continental, smoking cigarettes and sketching figures on the back of an envelope, while the trucks arrived and we went about the business of unloading the cattle. For the next six months we chased those steers from patch to patch of grass, wheat, and milo stubble. They got out. We went out in the middle of the night to put them back in. They got sick. We went to doctor them. Winter came and we moved them closer to the house, busting ice out of their water tanks and hauling grain silage to them every morning before school. All the while, the cattle market rose like a helium-filled balloon. Then one day in March or April, at the very peak of the market's curve, the trucks came again and took the cattle away. Once again Mr. Gable sat in his long black Lincoln, joined this time by our father, who sat a moment holding the check Mr. Gable had just cut him before shaking the man's hand and rejoining us in the gravel driveway.

"How much do you suppose that check is for?" I asked.

"Not nearly as much as Mr. Gable's end, that's for sure," Joe answered. "Dude probably made a hundred grand without ever taking off his John B. Stetson."

Dad must have heard these musings of ours, because as he headed off to his pickup to deposit the check in the glove box, I heard him say over his shoulder, "Yeah, well, you can lose just as much, and don't you forget it."

This was just Dad-speak, as far as I was concerned. From that day forward, regardless of what the old man said, I was an advocate of ranching over farming. The way I saw it, we'd be better off selling every acre of farm ground we owned and trading it straight across for grass and a feedlot of our own. But my father was too conservative for that. He also had farming in his blood in a way that I didn't and never would. And so we made the switch little by little. If we made some money farming, we'd put some of it into cows. If we made a little on cows, we'd put some of it into steers. Gradually it got to where we could think of ourselves as farmer-ranchers rather than simply farmers with a few head of cattle scattered here and there.

Then, a couple of years into the plan, Dad bought two hundred

Mexican steers at the low end of the market. As I recall, we had some pasture to get the cattle through the first part of the summer. When they'd eaten that, the plan was to shift them to a circle of Sudan grass we'd been irrigating like crazy. By the time the cattle were ready to be moved, the stuff was ten feet tall and thick as a jungle. We stretched a little one-wire electric fence around it, took a Bush Hog mower in there, cut an eight-foot "warning track" next to the fence, and set that herd of yearling steers loose to eat. I don't think those steers had ever seen a one-wire fence before, and I'm sure they'd never lived in a jungle. They were Llano steers from the desolate high plains of Texas. Most of them had never seen a man before they were loaded on trucks and brought north.

The smallest noise could set them off. At the time, we had a retired police dog, a German shepherd named Duke, living on the farm, and Duke had a tendency to make small noises. We'd be working in the shop and would feel the ground rumble, as if a train were coming down nearby tracks. We'd look up from our work and listen a minute, making out the distinct sound of hooves hitting hard ground, horns breaking through a thicket of Sudan. At this point I'd hurry out the shop door to watch the one-wire fence where it ran past our end of the pasture. There'd be a little wait, and then *twang!* The wire would jump up and down as if someone had shot an arrow off it. Then the wire would go slack, and good old Duke would emerge from the Sudan grass looking like he'd just performed some exceptional piece of police dog work, and had we seen it?

As a general rule, the steers wouldn't stop running until they'd put a good five miles between themselves and Duke. Everything on the farm ground to a halt until we managed to get them back between the wires. I've seen this process take days and several years off the lives of horses. More than once I've sat on a horse or in a pickup all night, trying to keep cattle off the road. When we finally managed to get all of the cattle back, my father, in his relentless optimism, would reassess the situation, deciding that all the steers really needed was an additional eight feet of warning track. They just didn't have enough room to come to a stop in between the time they came barreling out of the Sudan and the time they hit the fence. And so my brother Joe or I would fire up the Bush Hog mower and carve out another eight or sixteen feet. By the middle of winter, those steers had about sixty-four feet of warning track to stop in, but it didn't seem to make much difference.

There was a big snow coming, and this time we were taking no chances. We rounded up the steers and put them in a brand-new set of My-D-Handy corral panels next to the main shop building. What harm could come to them there?

I was in biology class, a sophomore in high school, when my father showed up in his battered pickup. Hooked to the back of the pickup was a stock trailer, and inside that, looking none too pleased, was a quarter horse named Sugar we'd recently acquired as an accessory to our ranching pretensions. I didn't say a word as I got into the truck, and my father didn't offer any explanations. Both of us knew what the deal was.

This time the steers had made it all the way into town, a good eight or nine miles from the farm. We saw the first of them coming up Wyatt Earp Boulevard, the main drag of the town, their tongues hanging out the sides of their mouths, their feet still at that dead Llano trot. Further up the street I could just make out the forms of two feedlot cowboys my father had hired to help round up the strays. Seeing them, he whipped the pickup and trailer sideways so that it blocked off most of the street, and I jumped out to unload Sugar. I could feel the eyes of townspeople staring at me from the windows of restaurants and bars as I mounted up. They were inside where it was nice and warm, and I was outside in the blowing snow with a bunch of renegade hamburger. There was a lesson to be learned in this, I thought.

Other steers were scattered here and there in snowbound parking lots and in front of stores. A few of them were found standing on the railroad tracks, as if waiting to catch the Southwest Chief to Albuquerque. A couple more stood huddled before the glass front doors of the Dodge House. As I rode up to get them, a waitress stuck her head out the door and yelled in a smoky voice, "These cows look like they could use a drink about now, ha ha ha."

I smiled weakly but did not join her in laughter. My adolescent dream of becoming a rich cattleman like John Gable was slowly departing from me like air from a punctured tire. If you'd asked me in that moment what I wanted to be when I grew up, I'd have gone as low as to say an accountant or a vice principal, anything to stay warm and outside the realm of cows and cowboys.

By early afternoon we'd rounded up the last of the steers and were pushing them back in the direction of the farm. A north wind was blasting down on us, and snow and ice flew through the air like buckshot. It got to where I couldn't see Sugar's ears or distinguish the snow-covered road from the ditches on either side of it. My hands and feet went numb in the cold, and my nose felt ready to fall off my face. Every once in a while, a steer or two would disappear into the ditch, and I'd have to ride Sugar in after them, the two of us sinking into the drifted snow all the way to my saddle horn. I'd look over at my father where he sat in his pickup with the window rolled down, snow blowing in on his face and hair. He would shrug as if to say, "What? You think this is bad? Son, I've seen far, far worse."

Halfway to the farm, we came upon the same feedlot where we used to buy bottle calves, and Dad motioned for us to stop and hold the cattle. Then as we stood there waiting and wondering what he'd do, he drove up to the feedlot office to have a talk with the manager. Five minutes later, some feedlot cowboys rode up on fresh horses and told us to start herding the cattle onto the snow-covered scale. We were leaving them for now and maybe forever.

"Thank God," I said aloud.

Later, as I was loading Sugar into the horse trailer, it occurred to me that the pen where the cattle stood bawling was the same one from which we'd rescued Big Ears all those years ago. I could still see him, neck deep in the muck, nothing but ears and attitude. Of course, it was to this same feedlot, a few years later, that Big Ears returned as a big, square-shouldered steer of eight or nine hundred pounds in order to be fattened for slaughter.

Did I feel a twinge of regret, remembering all that?

A little, yes. But I also felt proud. After all, by then we'd both fulfilled our separate destinies. Big Ears had reached the pinnacle of his life as a cow, and I'd reached mine as a cowboy, or so I thought at the time.

All that was left after that was the leaving.

—5—
The Fight

Word spread up and down the hallways of Dodge City Junior High, a school I'd attended for all of two weeks. A boy I'll call Lester Gutches, a burly, gap-toothed farm kid who'd been "held back" so many times he towered over the rest of us in the ninth grade, had been saying to anyone who'd listen that he was going to "kick that Rebein kid's ass."

At first I was more perplexed than scared by this news. Who the hell was Lester Gutches? How had he come to know my name? Did he really think I was going to fight him right there in the middle of the junior high?

For the previous eight years I'd attended Sacred Heart Cathedral, a Catholic grade school where everyone knew everyone else and fights were nonexistent. As a result, I found the whole idea of a guy I didn't know vowing to "kick my ass" hard to fathom. The only thing I could figure was that the public school kids were a little bent out of shape that twenty-five or so Catholic school boys had shown up on their turf in the last year of junior high and begun to compete with them for girlfriends and starting spots on the football and basketball teams. But Lester Gutches? People might as well have been talking about the Boogeyman.

It was football season, which meant there were ample opportunities before, during, and after practice for the other boys in ninth grade to razz me about the situation.

"You heard Gutches is after you, right?" one of my teammates, a skinny, bushy-haired boy named Eric Rouse, asked me while we were showering after practice.

"Yeah," I said, trying to sound cool about it.

"Don't fight him," Rouse said. "Everyone wants you to, but don't

41

fall for that shit. Gutches is a fucking animal. He's got nothing at all to lose, unlike you."

By then, all of the other guys in the shower were listening.

"Well, I won't pick a fight with him," I announced. "But I sure as hell won't run from him, either. Where would it end if I did?"

This was a line I'd heard from Robin Curtis, an older kid in my neighborhood, and I felt glad to have it to fall back on in this situation, even if I had no idea what it actually meant.

"Fuck that," Rouse responded. "That kind of thinking will get your ass killed. Gutches is a fucking *loser*, man. He carries knives and base-ball bats under the seats of that beat-up old car of his. You really want to let a guy like that take a crack at you?"

I shrugged dramatically and turned to let the hot water run down my back.

I was tall for my age, had played football, wrestled, and endured countless smack-downs at the hands of five older brothers—beatings I was quick to pass along to my younger brother, Paul. But none of this meant I knew how to handle myself in an actual fight. I'd never thrown or taken a real punch. Nor had I kicked anyone in the stomach or head or hidden behind a door outside shop class with a length of steel rod in my fist so that I could waylay a kid who'd made fun of the holes in my jeans, as Lester Gutches reportedly had done. To me, the whole idea of a fight was theoretical, as unreal in its way as sword swallowing or jumping out of an airplane with a parachute on my back.

But none of that mattered after Gutches officially threw down his challenge. It happened during lunch, of course. I was sitting at one of the back tables with a crowd of other guys from the football team when a tall, overweight kid in dirty Wranglers and work boots saun-tered into the room. "It's Gutches," someone whispered sharply. The boy paused a moment, squinting his washed-out blue eyes in an ef-fort to locate me, then walked straight up to where I was sitting. An acrid smell, a mixture of BO, cow shit, and diesel fuel, washed up at our table a second or two after he arrived. Though he was only fifteen years old, it was said that Gutches already worked fifty hours a week at a feedlot east of town. On days when he actually made it to school, he showed up in the same unwashed clothes he'd worn to work the day before. For guys like Lester Gutches, ninth grade was finishing school, the end of his formal education. As soon as his sixteenth birthday rolled around, he'd be out of there.

"You," he said, kicking the back leg of my chair with his boot.

"Me?" I asked dramatically, looking around at my friends and trying, unsuccessfully, to draw a laugh from them.

"Yeah, you," Gutches said, staring down at me. "Better get ready, cause I'm putting you on my to-do list. I ain't got time today, but I'm gonna kick your ass one of these days."

"Oh, well, thanks for letting me know," I said.

And with that, Gutches strode back out of the lunchroom, pausing only to spit a stream of tobacco juice into a trash can.

No sooner was he gone than the table buzzed with talk.

"You gonna take that shit, Rebein? . . . You can't let that dumb goat roper talk to you like that. . . . Better watch out, I'm telling you. . . . Dude is crazy."

For the first time, it was real to me. I was going to have to fight Lester Gutches. Either that or back down from him. No other path existed.

A few weeks before school started, I'd acquired a girlfriend, my first ever. Her name was Taryn, and she was a beautiful, dark-haired cheerleader, stepdaughter of one of the town doctors. She lived in a big Spanish-style house on a country lane west of town. In the evenings a couple of times a week, after football practice was over, I'd drive out there and lounge around with her on the shag carpeting of her sunken living room, kissing and pretending to watch TV, while her mother turned the pages of a newspaper in the next room.

"You're not going to fight Lester Gutches, are you?" she asked me one night.

"You heard about that?" I asked, surprised.

"Well, of course I *heard*," she said, sounding mildly insulted that I should doubt the extent to which she was clued into all of the gossip in the school. "Lester told me."

"Really? What did he say?"

"I can't repeat it," she said, playing coy.

"Why not?"

"The *language*," she said, nodding in the direction of the kitchen. "But I can whisper it in your ear, if you like."

"Sure," I said.

At this, she leaned into me, cupped both hands over my left ear, and said in a deep, breathy voice, "*Your boyfriend is a P-U-S-S-Y.*"

"You're kidding me, right?" I asked.

She shook her head, eyes boring into mine. A sort of weird electric current ran between us. We kissed, and she opened her mouth for me for the first time ever. I moved my hand to the front of the tight pink sweater she was wearing, but she caught my wrist expertly and guided it back down to my side. "No, no, not yet," she said.

"When?"

"Who knows?" she said, laughing.

An hour later, I drove home in a state of hot confusion. *She's egging me on,* I thought. *She wants me to fight him, just like everyone else. If I don't, she'll look bad in front of all of the other cheerleaders.*

I didn't blame her for any of this. In a weird way, it made her more desirable in my eyes. Here was a girl whose love had to be earned. It was thrilling to think about that. It was thrilling to think about a lot of other things, too.

Days passed, and the tension at school reached a crescendo of sorts. Gutches began driving his beat-up Chevelle around and around the football field during practice, pausing every once in a while to throw the car into neutral and rev the engine. Everyone on the field, coaches and players alike, would look up, at which point he'd throw the car into gear and peel out.

"Who is that?" asked our head coach, an old bachelor everyone called "Jungle Bob" on account of the pith helmet he habitually wore to practice.

"It's Gutches," one of the guys said. "He's after Rebein."

"Robert, is that true?" Jungle Bob asked, looking mildly concerned.

I shook my head, embarrassed that the whole thing had come up yet again. "I don't know. Anyway, I'm not worried about it."

"Well, you ought to be," he said. "We've got an undefeated season going here, and the last thing we need is for our starting outside line-backer to go and get himself injured in a fight."

"Okay, okay," I said.

"So you'll handle this the right way? No fistfights or anything like that?"

"Yeah," I lied. "Can we get back to practicing?"

But I knew I had to do something. If I kept waiting, the situation would continue to balloon until it got completely out of control. It was only a matter of time before Gutches caught me off guard somewhere and cold-cocked me, the way he'd done that other kid outside of shop class.

I took my problem to Robin Curtis, my neighborhood's expert on such matters. Talking it over, we agreed that the thing to do was to hit Gutches before he had a chance to hit me. However, we disagreed about tactics. My idea was to take Gutches straight to his back with a double-leg takedown and then figure things out from there.

"You're going to *wrestle* him?" Robin laughed. "That's your plan? A guy who outweighs you by forty or fifty pounds?"

"You got a better idea?" I asked.

"You better hope I do," Robin said, shaking his head.

The plan was simple, and we practiced it over and over, until I had every part of it down pat. As Gutches walked up to me in the hallway or cafeteria (we'd already determined that the fight had to take place on school grounds, where teachers could stop it if things got out of hand), I was to hold my arms down at my sides as though I had no in-tention of fighting. Then when he got close enough, I'd kick him once in the shin. "More of a tap than a kick," Robin explained. "The idea is to make him react, not to hurt him." I would follow that up immediately with a fist to the nose. "Remember," Robin reminded me over and over. "You're not aiming to punch him in the *face*. You're aiming to punch him in the *nose*. If you aim for his face, you'll hit his chin or something. If you aim for his nose, bam, you'll lay him out."

"You really think it'll work?" I asked.

"Hell, yes, it'll work," Robin said. "And if it doesn't, well, run."

The next time Gutches showed up at school, I sent word through a friend from Sacred Heart that I wanted to meet him in the lobby in front of the library between third and fourth periods. Following Robin's instructions, I didn't say I wanted to fight him. Instead, I made it sound like I wanted to talk. After all, I didn't want Gutches hatching any plans of his own. Word of the showdown spread quickly. Throughout my first couple of classes, people I didn't even know passed me notes saying things like "Kick his ass!" and "Get him!" I couldn't believe these people. It wasn't like they cared about me or were on my side. They just wanted to see a fight.

Then the end of third period rolled around, and I took up my place in the center of the lobby, halfway between the principal's office and the glass-windowed library. The place was packed with kids milling around pretending to do anything but what they were really doing, which was waiting to see a fight. Then the buzz picked up at the far end of the hall, where the shop classes were, and I knew Gutches was on his way. I could feel my right foot tapping involuntarily on the tiled floor. *Tap, bam,* I repeated to myself. *Tap, bam, tap, bam, tap, bam.*

Finally Gutches himself appeared. He was alone, as usual, and walked with a kind of limping shuffle. *Probably got kicked by a steer at the feedlot,* I thought, and for a brief moment I felt sorry for the guy. After all, he had no idea what was about to hit him. But then, as he got closer, I saw that he had a faint smile on his face, his pale eyes seeming to dilate with pleasure, and all thought of feeling sorry for him left me.

Four steps away, three steps, two. . . .

"Well, well," he began in his nasal drawl.

Here goes nothing, I thought.

Tap, bam!

The kick to his shin made Gutches stumble forward, and he walked right into the punch that followed. I could feel the cartilage in his nose crunch between the middle knuckles of my fist. Blood began to pour into his mouth and down his chin. He took a big step back, stunned by what had happened.

"Holy shit! Did you see that?" someone yelled. "Rebein broke his nose!"

A few seconds later, both the principal and vice principal came running out of their offices and grabbed Gutches and me by our necks. "Everyone clear the halls! Clear the halls!" the principal yelled. "Did you hear me? Clear these halls now!"

The blood continued to pour from Gutches's nose as we were dragged into the school's administrative offices. He pulled up the front of his T-shirt to catch it, but his eyes were on me the whole time, and it seemed to me that he was smiling, laughing almost. Then he was taken off to the nurse's office by the principal, while the vice principal dragged me into an adjoining room.

"What in God's name happened out there?" the vice principal asked.

"I hit him."

"Well, that's pretty darned obvious," the man said. "The question is *why* did you hit him?"

I looked up then, seeing the vice principal as if for the first time. He was short, bald, and compactly built, with muscular arms covered over in thick black hair. An assistant football coach for the high school team, he was bound to side with me over a guy like Lester Gutches, no matter what had really happened.

"I don't know," I said. "He was bothering me."

"Well, just between you and me," the man continued, "I'd say he got just about what he deserved. What do you think?"

"I don't know," I said. "I guess so."

Ten minutes later, after Gutches's nose had stopped bleeding, we were brought together in the principal's office, where we were asked to "shake hands and make it up." We did as we were told, Gutches laughing through the whole thing. I stared at the damage I'd done to his face. The skin beneath both his eyes was turning a yellowish purple. As for his nose, there was no question it was broken.

"You know the penalty for fighting in school," the principal said. "Five swats or a Saturday detention. It's your choice."

"I'll take the swats," Gutches said without hesitation.

"What about you?" the principal asked, turning to me.

"Detention."

This brought a laugh from Gutches, but I didn't care. Unlike him, I had no job to get to, and a couple of hours of homework in the school library wasn't all that different from my usual Saturday routine. Besides, there was no way I was going to let some middle-aged guy with hairy arms whale on me with a wooden paddle.

I enjoyed a brief period of school yard fame in the days immediately following the fight. Girls I didn't know slipped notes into my locker, and boys slapped me on the back as I passed them in the hall. Even Taryn was affected, letting me kiss her longer and touch her in places that previously had been off-limits.

"Everyone thinks you're a tough guy, fucking Billy Jack or something," my friend Eric from the football team observed. "But you know this shit's not over, right? You know Gutches is gonna come at you again sooner or later, right?"

"Yeah, I know," I said.

Meanwhile, Lester Gutches himself was nowhere to be seen. He was sick, or waiting for his nose to heal, or busy at the feed yard, or had been thrown into "juvy" yet again—there was no end to the theories. At the same time, his absence did nothing to stop or slow gossip about the impending "rematch," as people began to call it. At least

once a day, in classes as different as English and Shop and P.E., someone, usually some skinny kid with bad skin, would slide up to where I
was sitting and say, "Man, I'd hate to be you," or "Look out, cause old
Gutches is gonna tear you to pieces when he gets back."

"Really?" I'd say. "Where did you hear that?"

"Shit, everybody knows it's true," the kid would answer.

Sometimes a more sinister prediction reached me, something
about Gutches and a baseball bat, Gutches and a lead pipe, Gutches
and a pair of nunchakus or brass knuckles he had made in Shop class.
The worst of it came when a kid in my Shop class, Rob Reynolds,
suggested Gutches might decide to make me "his bitch" after he was
through kicking my ass. "He's into that stuff," Reynolds said, laughing.
"You think it's bad now when he hates you. Just you wait until he starts
to *like* you." At the time, I had no idea what Reynolds was talking
about. Only later, when Robin Curtis explained the concept to me, did
I begin to understand. I was stunned. For the first time since I'd heard
Gutches was after me, I began to get a little scared.

Then, a week or so after he disappeared, Gutches made a dramatic
reappearance. This time it was not at school or one of my practices but
right smack in the middle of a Friday night high school football game.
In those days, ninth grade was not yet a part of high school, which
is why I was not down on the field myself. Instead, I was high in the
stands with Taryn, the two of us huddled together against the wind
and the cold. I'd loaned her my new letter jacket, and my arm was
thrown over her shoulder, my torso covered by nothing more than a
flannel shirt. It was through the thin, checkered fabric of this shirt that
I felt the first prick of Gutches's knife. The second I felt the pressure of
the blade—just below my left lung—I knew exactly what it was. Still,
I didn't turn around for another second or two. Instead, I drew Taryn
closer to me, pulling her face to my chest so she wouldn't see. Only
then did I glance over my shoulder at where Gutches sat, by himself
as always, elbows on his knees, the long blade of a hunting knife held
delicately in both hands.

"Hi ya," he mouthed at me obscenely.

I don't remember what, if anything, I said in response. All I really recall is how *stupid stupid stupid* I felt for letting Gutches get that close to me without seeing any of it coming. But it was weird. Although the situation was clearly a dangerous one, I was less worried about getting hurt—or even Taryn getting hurt, for that matter—than I was about being embarrassed in front of her. Even as Gutches began to twist the knife lightly, its tip breaking through the fabric of my shirt to touch the skin of my back, embarrassment and how to avoid it was my paramount concern. Holding Taryn closer with each passing moment, I racked my brains for what I could do to get out of the situation without losing face or getting stabbed. However, no plan came to mind, and in the end it was Gutches himself who bailed me out. After failing to get a rise out of me or Taryn—she told me later that she'd known the whole time he was back there, had, in fact, found parts of it to be "exciting"—he simply grew bored and stood up to leave.

"We'll be seeing you soon," he whispered in my ear.

It was not long after this that I experienced one of those phantasms of terror that are so much a part of growing up. Ever since the knife incident at the football game, I'd been troubled by the idea that Gutches would show up somewhere I wasn't expecting him and ambush me. For the first time in my life, I began to look over my shoulder, pausing before I entered stairwells or rounded corners, always half-expecting Gutches to leap out at me like some life-sized jack-in-the-box, a hideous grin animating his red, sweaty face. In my mind, he'd been transformed into a monster, one of those terrible beings that populate fairy tales. I just knew that sooner or later he'd "get me," and I both dreaded this outcome and wished it would hurry up and happen so I could quit thinking and worrying about it all the time.

It was after football practice, three or four days after the knife incident, and I'd stayed behind in the locker room to ice an ankle I turned running wind sprints. It had been an unusually warm afternoon for early October, and someone had propped the locker room's back door open with a cement block. It was through this open door that I was visited by the heavy rumble of Gutches gunning his old Chevy in the street outside. *VROOM, bump-bump-bump-bump-bump-bump-bump, VROOOOOOM, bump-bump-bump-bump, VRR-ROOOOOOOMM!* Hearing this, I felt my stomach drop and the muscles around my heart constrict.

It's him, I thought. *He's waiting for me outside. What if he has a knife—or worse? Why didn't I think to bring some kind of weapon for protection? What a goddamn fool I am!*

I was alone. All of the coaches and other players had gone home for the day. Even the equipment managers and the trainers had left. Again and again I heard the terrible *VROOOM* of Gutches's engine in the street. I heard it as I dressed, as I slowly put away my practice uniform, as I struggled to get a tennis shoe on over my swollen foot. Each time the sound recurred, I felt a little more desperate and trapped. Then, as I was adjusting the laces on my shoes for the fifteenth or twentieth time, the noise stopped abruptly. I stood up and listened harder, but all remained quiet. Had Gutches grown tired of waiting and left, or had he merely cut the engine to save gas and was waiting for me now in the parking lot next to my car? I gathered what was left of my courage and went outside.

What I saw from the steps of the locker room was almost too good to be true. All was clear. The whole parking lot was empty except for my yellow Mustang II, and the street beyond that was clear, too—no sign at all of Gutches or his blue Chevy. With my heart beating fast, I hobbled across the lot, threw my bags in the back seat of the Mustang, and peeled out of there.

Home was a mile away. I was halfway there when I spotted a blue Chevy two blocks behind me and gaining fast. I turned a quick left onto a side street, then gunned it down an alley and made a couple more quick turns, checking my rearview mirror all the while to see if Gutches was still following or if by some miracle I had managed to lose him. Did he know where I lived? If so, why follow me home from practice? These and other thoughts absorbed me as I approached the wide driveway in front of my parents' house. Both doors on our four-car garage stood open, but I had no intention of parking there. Instead I drove my car right up to the back door of the house, cut the engine, and hobbled the last six or seven feet on my sore ankle. In a matter of seconds I was through the back door and down the steps and across the basement floor to my bedroom at the back of the house.

Once there, I sat tensely on the edge of my bed, listening and waiting, my heart beating loudly in my ears. A minute or two passed, and I was beginning to calm down when I heard it again, the same as I had in the locker room. *VROOM, bump-bump-bump, VROOOOOOM, bump-bump, VRRROOOOOOOMM!* I felt the blood go cold in my veins as my mind supplied a picture of Gutches sitting in his beat-up Chevy in the driveway to my house, grinning stupidly as he continued to rev the engine. It was five or five-thirty in the afternoon, too early for my father or any of my older brothers to be home. As for my mother, she was probably at the store, picking up something for dinner.

This is it, I thought. *I'm gonna have to fight Gutches on his terms this time. No more surprising him with a sucker punch. No more vice principal to jump in and stop things before they get out of hand.*

With a kind of dread stoicism, I headed upstairs to meet my doom. Halfway there, I doubled back to ransack a knife drawer in the kitchen, coming up finally with a dull butcher's knife. At the back door, I paused a moment to collect myself—the *VROOOM* of Gutches's engine was louder than ever—then stepped outside.

Stooped over his Kawasaki 900, with one hand on the throttle and the other on the bike's choke, was my older brother, Alan. *VROOM, bump-bump-bump, VROOOOOOM, bump-bump, VRR-ROOOOOOOMM!*

I sat down hard on the steps, letting the knife fall to the ground.

Which was worse, I wondered, as a mixture of relief and disappointment washed over me: thinking Lester Gutches was outside my house waiting to kick my ass, or coming out to discover that he wasn't there after all and that the suspense would only continue? Sitting there, my hands shaking uncontrollably, I remembered a short story I'd read about a condemned man, a political prisoner, who gets dragged in front of a firing squad. Then, inexplicably, after he's already prepared himself to die, the whole thing is called off, and he's dragged back to his cell. He's traumatized, overcome with despair. *I prepared myself to die*, he thinks, *but the shots never came. Now what?*

I didn't understand the story when I read it, but I understood it now.

I understood, too, that the situation with Gutches wouldn't fade away or die down of its own accord. Something definite would have to happen, something that would either satisfy Gutches or scare him off for good. What that something was, I still didn't know. All I knew was that, from my point of view, it couldn't happen soon enough.

The next day I lurked in the vicinity of Gutches's locker until he finally showed up between second and third periods. Although it was plenty warm in the school, he had on a dirty hoodie and a jean jacket, as if he might have to leave for work at the feedlot any moment. "Hey, dick brains," he said to me, smiling weakly. "I'm surprised you have the guts to show your face after that chicken shit you pulled at the football game."

"Whatever," I said, clenching and unclenching my fists nervously. "If you wanna fight again, you can meet me at the Kwik Shop on Central right after football practice. If you don't, that's cool, too. I don't care. I'm just sick of this shit, and I want to be done with it."

"Oh, yeah?" Gutches responded, pausing to spit into a paper cup he kept on the shelf of his otherwise empty locker. "What if I'm not sick of it? What if I'm just getting started?"

"Tough," I said. "This is it. You can beat the shit out of me or whatever you want to do. I'm done, that's all."

Then something very strange happened. Instead of laughing or making fun of me, Gutches grew quiet and serious and said to me in a shy, almost friendly voice, "Your dad runs cattle, don't he?"

"Yeah," I said. "So?"

"Nothing," he responded. "A load of his yearlings came in at the feedlot, and I noticed the name, that's all."

Then the bell for third period rang, and he slammed the locker shut and turned to leave. I stood there and watched him go, still perplexed by the bizarre exchange of words.

"See you after practice," he called over his shoulder.

"All right," I called back.

I'm not proud of what happened next, and yet if I were faced with the same situation again, I can't say that I would do anything differently.

Our practice that day was a light one, it being the day before an out-of-town game. As a result, I arrived at the Kwik Shop fifteen or twenty minutes early, and I brought a considerable entourage along with me—the whole ninth grade football team, more or less. Gutches, meanwhile, arrived alone, and by the time he got there, the parking lot in front of the convenience store was so full he had to park on a hill a half block down the street. I stood off to the side of the store, fifteen or twenty guys at my back, watching as Gutches parked the old Chevy and lumbered up the hill. There was something almost pathetic about the way he walked along in his work boots, hands in his pockets, head down. I can see that now, looking back on these events across a space of thirty years and more, but I don't think I saw it then. I was too caught up in my own problems to imagine his.

Having reached the top of the hill, Gutches shuffled up to where I stood, hands still in his pockets, and offered me that odd smile of his. "Looks like you brought friends," he said.

"I did," I answered, nodding, and immediately I felt ashamed about having ganged up on him in this way. At the same time, there was no going back on any of it now. "Go ahead," I told him. "Take your best shot. It's the last one you're ever going to get."

I had my hands down at my sides, the same as the first time we fought, but otherwise my intentions couldn't have been more different. Rather than hit Gutches, I was going to let him hit me. That was it, the extent of my plan. I was going to even the thing out one way or another.

When he saw what I was up to, all Gutches could do was laugh and shrug his massive shoulders. It was a sucker's choice he had to make, after all. If he hit me and I did nothing to defend myself, the whole football team would jump him and exact a revenge many of them had been waiting for years to accomplish. If he didn't hit me, he'd look foolish and weak. Worse, it would be like he'd wasted all of our time.

"Well?" I asked, almost taunting him now.

At this Gutches grinned widely, bent sharply at the knees, and faked a right fist to my stomach. I reacted with a hard flinch—even the guys behind me took a step back—and this gave Gutches the opening he was looking for. He threw his head back and laughed, then said in a bored, even voice, "Sorry, guys. I'd like to hang around and play games with you all, but I've got to get to work."

And with that, he walked back down the hill to his car, got in, and drove off.

You can bet that all the guys I'd dragged out of the locker room that day didn't let me forget the extent to which I'd "pussied out" and wasted their time. "Man, you call that a fight?" they said. "That was fucking pathetic!"

It was pathetic. I agreed completely. But it was also over, and for that I felt considerable relief. Without throwing a punch, I'd ended the whole thing, and by the following week, a completely different drama absorbed the school, this one about a girl and a broom closet and certain sexual favors she was supposedly handing out.

Looking back, the thing that sticks with me the most about the whole episode is not the single punch that was thrown or the terror I felt when I thought Gutches had followed me home. It was that image of him trudging up the hill by himself to face a foe surrounded by friends he didn't have. It was supposed to be me, the newcomer, the Catholic schoolboy, who was the outcast in that last year of junior high before we all headed off to the high school down the hill. Instead, I'd blended right in with the public school kids in a way that Gutches, who'd grown up among them, could never hope to do.

Not long after our showdown at the Kwik Shop, Gutches quit school for good and went to work full-time at the feedlot. In years to come, I'd run into him in different bars around town, and each time he'd corner me and start acting like we were the best of friends, throwing a beefy arm around my neck and ribbing me about breaking his nose.

"Do you remember?" he'd ask. "All that blood running down my shirt?"

"Oh, I remember," I'd say, counting the moments until it was safe for me to leave him standing there and rejoin my friends at the opposite end of the bar.

—6—
Hoops, Happiness, Pistol Pete, and Me

Like all hoop dreams of the small-town white-boy variety, this one begins in a darkening driveway in the farm belt, where a boy, twelve or thirteen years old, his head a mop of brown curls, shoes scuffed and tight at the toes, shoots basket after basket on a fan-shaped goal his father built out of salvaged irrigation pipe.

As he shoots, the boy repeats under his breath certain talismanic phrases: "fingertips," "elbow in," "high release," "follow through." Each shot is identical to the one that came before it—or as close to identical as the boy can make it. First, the ball is brought up until it is "locked and loaded" above the right shoulder, both wrist and elbow forming separate 90-degree angles. Then, with a slight bend of the knees, the ball is brought higher still, into the "pocket" just above the boy's right ear. Finally, it is flipped up in a "rainbow arch" toward the rim, the boy's index finger extending to its highest point of release, at which point the wrist flips over and the fingers point down, in a position shooters call "hand in the cookie jar."

Throughout the shooting motion, the boy's eyes never leave the iron hoop. Only when the ball passes through, splashing against the back of the net to create a satisfying *swish* sound, does the boy follow his shot, catching the ball on the rebound and pivoting to shoot again.

Load. Lift. Release. *Swish.*

And then another.

Load. Lift. Release. *Swish.*

Each time he hears that *swish*, the boy's eyes dilate with happiness. For him, in this moment, there is no better sound in all the world.

When I was that boy, growing up in western Kansas, the undisputed king of my basketball universe was a lanky, mop-headed guard named "Pistol" Pete Maravich. In those days, Pistol Pete played for the New Orleans Jazz, an expansion NBA franchise that rarely got to play on national TV. Indeed, I could count on one hand the number of times I'd seen Pistol Pete play in an actual game. My knowledge of him came from other sources: gossip, the hearsay of those who claimed to have "seen the Pistol in his prime," and certain prerecorded halftime segments like "Red on Roundball," an instructional series hosted by the legendary Boston Celtics coach Red Auerbach. Pistol Pete was a regular on Red's show, appearing on such segments as "Red on Roundball: Passing," "Red on Roundball: The Corner Position," "Red on Roundball: Alley-Oop," "Red on Roundball: Dribbling," and, most famously, "Red on Roundball: Ball-Handling Drills." In these brief segments, a bald, potbellied Auerbach expounded on various aspects of the pro game while one or two NBA stars (Pistol Pete, Dr. J, David Thompson, Jo Jo White), wearing the ridiculously tight shorts of that era, did their best to demonstrate what he was talking about.

Although Pistol Pete was a fantastic shooter and an even better passer, he usually appeared on Red's show to demonstrate his preternatural ball-handling skills—skills he'd acquired through countless hours practicing a sequence of drills he called "homework basketball." Bearing colorful names like "Pretzel," "Flap Jack," or "Bullet Ricochet," these drills invariably contained some parlor-trick element like spinning a ball on an upturned finger or dribbling two balls at once . . . while blindfolded.

"Pete Maravich," Red narrated in his thick Brooklyn accent. "In my opinion, one of the great, great guards in basketball. *Did not get that way by accident!* He worked. He trained. He developed. And *that's* why he's Pete Maravich!"

I remember lying in front of my parents' Curtis Mathis in the basement of our house on Cedar Street, a red-white-and-blue basketball beneath my chin, thinking confidently to myself, *Yes, and that's gonna be me someday, too. Old Red's gonna say the same things about me.*

The most memorable of Pistol Pete's nongame TV appearances came during CBS's coverage of the 1978 All-Star Game in Atlanta, where the Pistol, unleashing his entire arsenal of trick shots, defeated "Bubbles" Hawkins, George "Iceman" Gervin, and Bob McAdoo on his way to winning that year's H-O-R-S-E competition. In one sequence, Pistol Pete passed the ball behind his back and under his right thigh before flipping it, left-handed, off the glass and into the basket. The whole sequence was so improbable, so ridiculous, and yet so *practiced,* that all McAdoo could do in response was to shake his head and ask, "Can I see that one *on replay?*"

That was always the way with Pistol Pete. Everything he did seemed to cry out for a replay. And yet there was something else there, something that my twelve-year-old self did not pick up on but that my middle-aged self, watching the segment on YouTube, could see all too clearly. The compulsive drive and hangdog sadness of the man. The way, when he missed a shot, he slammed the ball hard against the floor, berating himself under his breath with a single, dagger-like word. "*Choke!*"

"What's *that* all about?" I had to wonder.

Socrates, the father of Western philosophy, has little to say on the subject of human happiness. Several of Socrates's disciples, however, do speak to the subject, and their separate insights present a veritable quilt of contrasting opinions. Aristippus of Cyrene, sometimes called the "father of hedonism," held that happiness was to be discovered in the senses—in external pleasure. Another of Socrates's students, Antisthenes, believed that the opposite was true: happiness was to be found not in sensual fulfillment but rather in an inner peace achieved through a life of simplicity, modesty, and virtue. For his part, Plato, the greatest of all of Socrates's pupils, divided the human soul into three parts—reason, will, and desire. Only when all three parts of the soul are in balance, Plato wrote, can we humans hope to achieve something remotely resembling happiness.

Pleasure through the senses. Inner peace. Balance.

Are these the keys to human happiness? And if so, what does any of them have to do with basketball?

Pistol Pete Maravich was the product of the steel towns south of Pittsburgh, a region famously described as "hell with the lid taken off." From the first, Pete's father, Petar "Press" Maravich, the son of immigrant steelworkers from Serbia and later a barnstorming professional basketball player and a college coach, had set out to make young Pete a basketball phenomenon, the "best who ever played the game." By the age of seven, Pete was practicing eight or nine hours a day—dribbling, shooting, throwing behind-the-back passes at a big X painted on the basement wall. Press called these drills "homework basketball," and most days it was the only kind of homework young Pete Maravich ever did.

Showing Pete off at basketball camps across the country, Press got rave reviews from other coaches, who marveled at the crazy things Pete could do with a basketball. In fact, the only coach who demurred was John Wooden of UCLA. How many hours went into learning so much bizarre, useless stuff? Wooden wanted to know. Wouldn't the boy be better off learning fundamentals like proper footwork or how to play defense? At other times, Wooden would shake a bony finger at Press. "You're putting too much pressure on one boy," he'd say. Not that Press ever listened. He was Earl Woods before there was a Tiger, Mike Agassi before there was an Andre, Marv Marinovich before there was a Todd.

As for Pete himself, he was the original gym rat. Basketball was like a drug to him or some kind of deep, transcendental meditation. Even the repetitive drills provided a high of sorts, a release that was impossible to get any other way. As Pete's childhood friend Jim Sutherland would say years later of the times the two of them broke into the Clemson gymnasium in the middle of the night to play, "If you could pick anything you wanted to do, any place you wanted to be, that was it. It was heaven."

Hoops. Happiness. Heaven.

By the time he was in eighth grade—gangly, prepubescent, maybe five-six and 85 pounds—Pete was starting on the varsity basketball team at Daniel High School in Central, South Carolina. By the time he was a sophomore, he was the focal point of the team—bringing the ball up court, throwing wild, behind-the-back passes, floating into the lane to fire the ball from his hip "like a gunslinger." After an early season game in which he poured in 33 points, a writer from the local paper enthused about how "Pistol Pete" Maravich had utterly dominated the game.

Pistol Pete. Fifteen years old and already he had his own professional-sounding moniker. Even his father used it. "Hell," Press would tell anyone who'd listen, "if you think Pistol Pete is good now, just you wait. That kid is the future of basketball."

My own father was nothing at all like Press Maravich—a fact I secretly held against him. While my father liked sports well enough and had even played fullback at St. Mary of the Plains College back in the 1950s, his focus during the years I was growing up was squarely on farming, ranching, and the salvage yard business he ran with his older brother, not on the childhood athletic pursuits of kids like me or my brothers. He made sure we had the equipment we needed to play, and he even came to our games when he could fit them into his work schedule, but he did not push, coach, or offer advice. And when one of my brothers decided to give up sports altogether after the eighth grade in order to pursue an interest in hot rods and woodworking, well, he was fine with that, too. Sports were our deal, not his.

From any early age, I participated in a wide range of sports—baseball, football, basketball, wrestling, track. Each season had its own special aroma, its own set of pleasures and possibilities. Whatever sport I happened to be playing at the time, *that* sport was always my favorite.

Then, toward the end of seventh grade, my priorities began to change. I started to rank the sports I played according to how good I was (or thought I was) at them, and a year or two after that, I began to weed out what I saw as the less promising ones. The first sport to be eliminated was wrestling, as it conflicted directly with basketball. Next to go was track, then baseball. By the time I entered ninth grade, I was down to just two sports, football and basketball, and there could be no question which of the two I was better at playing. While I was good enough to start both ways in football, I was maybe the ninth or tenth best player on a thirty-man roster. But basketball was a different story. I had a special knack or affinity for it, a will to score points and to take over games. My destiny, as I saw it, was to star on the Dodge City Red Demons before moving on to the Kansas Jayhawks and, eventually, to Auerbach's Boston Celtics.

In pursuit of these goals, I dedicated myself to a daily regimen of dribbling, ball-handling, and shooting drills ("homework basketball"). I carried a basketball with me wherever I went and became known for challenging older kids to games of 21, Round the World, H-O-R-S-E, or one-on-one. In time I became a decent ball handler and developed a reliable outside shot as well. However, my stock-in-trade as a player was always my drive series.

As its name would suggest, a "drive series" is a series of moves (with an almost infinite number of variations within the series) designed to get the offensive player past his defender and to the rim, where the resulting shot is either a layup or a quick pull-up jumper. The top five or six moves in my drive series were (1) the jabstep-and-go, (2) the head-fake-and-go, (3) the jabstep-crossover-and-go, (4) the jabstep-reverse-spin-pull-up, (5) the head-fake-jabstep-crossover-and-go, and finally (6) the head-fake-jabstep-reverse-spin-fade-away. I practiced these moves compulsively. After all, the goal was not simply to become proficient or "good" at these moves; the goal was to become *unstoppable*.

The summer after my ninth grade year, I attended the Ted Owens Jayhawk Basketball Camp on the campus of the University of Kansas in Lawrence. I was a lanky, six-foot forward with a workman-like jump shot and a series of moves off the dribble that were difficult to stop. At the end of the weeklong camp, I was named to the 15-and-under All-Star team and got to play a game against a 16-and-under team in historic Allen Fieldhouse, named after Forrest "Phog" Allen, the "father of basketball coaching," who'd learned his trade from none other than Dr. James Naismith, the inventor of the game and KU's first coach.

Who can say why sometimes we perform poorly and without inspiration, yet at other times we catch fire and play far above our natural abilities? All I know is that in this particular game, everything I threw at the basket went in. I racked up 18 points in the first quarter alone, and the streak didn't stop there. Late in the game, just for the hell of it, I pulled up thirty feet from the basket, gave a head fake, and waited until the opposing team's point guard crashed into me, at which point I bounced off him and threw up a prayer of a shot. Falling theatrically to the ground, I slid on my butt across the polished hardwood of the field house, my shooting arm still raised, index finger pointing down, "hand in the cookie jar." The shot hit nothing but net, and my fellow campers went wild. Half an hour later, Jo Jo White, a former All-American at Kansas and the starting point guard for the Boston Celtics, presented me with a trophy with an engraving that read "Outstanding Jayhawk Player."

I was ecstatic about this success, but not surprised. Later that summer, I ran into the high school football coach in a sporting goods store in downtown Dodge City, and when he asked me what my plans were for the fall, I replied, "No more football for me. I'm gonna concentrate on basketball."

"Really?" Coach Masters asked, raising his eyebrows as if to question why anyone would make such a decision. "Well, good luck to you then. Just remember: if you ever change your mind, you can always come see me."

Fat chance of that happening, I thought at the time.

St. Augustine of Hippo, who published a famous treatise on the subject of happiness during the Christian Middle Ages, taught that the
good or happy life was to be achieved not by indulging in external
pleasures (Augustine himself had exhausted that route during a riot-
ous youth), or even by seeking a Platonic balance of reason, will, and
desire, but rather by the difficult act of "living in God." Since God was
responsible for all good things, Augustine argued, without God there
could be no possibility of happiness.

Augustine's way of thinking radically simplified the whole question of human happiness, preparing the way for more pessimistic phi-
losophers like Arthur Schopenhauer, who believed that human life
was little more than a "vale of tears" characterized by alternating bouts
of boredom and suffering. If all happiness depends on God, so the rea-
soning went, and man, in the ultimate act of hubris, has declared God
to be "dead," then isn't the whole question of happiness dead as well?

No happiness without God. No God. Ergo, no happiness.

The tidiness of this syllogism is second only to the despair it occasions in the hearts of all who consider it deeply.

Pistol Pete's first choice among the colleges that recruited him was
West Virginia University, where the great Jerry West had played. He
might have gone there, too, observes Mark Kriegel in *Pistol: The Life
of Pete Maravich,* if only his father, Press, hadn't been offered the head
coaching position at Louisiana State University, where the assumption
was that the two of them, father and son, would come to Baton Rouge
as a "package deal."

"LSU, that's a football school," Pete complained when he heard
about the deal. "They probably don't even have a gym down there."

"You go to West Virginia," Press announced angrily, "you don't
ever bring your ass into my house again."

Back and forth it went, father accusing son of treason, son accusing father of profiteering, until finally Pete came up with a compro-
mise of sorts. "If I'm going to LSU, you got to buy me a car."

"Car, my ass," Press said.

But he bought it all the same.

It was at LSU that the legend of Pistol Pete was established in the national consciousness. The elements of the legend were these: individual stats of a kind no player had ever put up before (3,667 points over a three-year career, an average of more than 44 points per game); a style of play that was flamboyant to the point of outrageousness (shots from half court, no-look passes, displays of ball handling straight out of the Harlem Globetrotters); finally a modern "Age of Aquarius" look that included mop-top hair and wool socks with the elastic removed so that they flopped around his ankles.

Before Pistol Pete arrived on campus, few people at LSU would have thought of attending a basketball game. But all that changed in Pistol's very first game as a freshman, when he put up 50 points to go along with 14 rebounds and 11 assists against Southeastern Louisiana College. It was "show time," and the entire LSU offense was built around a single idea: get Pete the ball and let him score. Wins and losses were almost irrelevant, and indeed, the Tigers lost more than their share, going 8-10 in the SEC in Pete's sophomore season, 7-11 in his junior season.

Gradually, though, the pressure to put up bigger and bigger numbers began to take a toll on Pete. The game he loved and that had given him so much pleasure as a boy came to feel like a job—and a high-pressure one at that. To relieve the pressure, he drank, throwing down beer after beer until he would pass out and have to be carried home by teammates, many of whom resented his ball-hogging ways. During the Tigers' run to the NIT semis in 1970, Pistol Pete played with a colossal hangover the entire tournament. "His eyes," one teammate remembered, "looked like two piss holes in a snow pile." In his final game, a 101–79 loss to Marquette, Pete, playing half-drunk from the night before, shot just 4 for 13 from the field and managed "only" 20 points. The pain caused by this failure was no less intense for having been self-inflicted. "My stupidity not only contributed to a loss," he later wrote, "but humiliated my dad, and that was unbearable."

The years 1976 to 1980 were a high-water mark for basketball in Dodge City. The high school team, the Red Demons, made several deep runs in a prestigious midseason tournament called the Tournament of Champions (TOC, for short) and was routinely ranked among the top five teams in the state. The team's best player during these years was a long-range bomber named Steve Reid who would later achieve an odd but lasting fame as the player shooting a free throw for Purdue when Indiana's Bobby Knight went on his infamous chair-throwing spree.

However, the glory years of Dodge City basketball were all but finished by the time I entered high school in the fall of 1980. The team's longtime coach retired abruptly as soon as Steve Reid graduated, and the new coach was an outsider to Dodge City by the name of "Rocket Rod" Kirschner. As it happened, Rocket Rod had been working the Jayhawk basketball camp the summer before when Jo Jo White presented me with the Outstanding Jayhawk Player award. I remember how he came up to me after the awards ceremony, a stooped, rangy figure with wavy black hair and an eyes-half-shut smile that made you wonder if he wasn't perhaps laughing at some private joke.

"You mind me asking how tall your dad is?"

"My dad? I don't know. Five-eleven, maybe?"

"What about your mom?"

"Wow. I couldn't say. Five-six?"

He smiled his closed-mouth smile. "What about brothers or cousins, aunts or uncles? Any of them taller than you are?"

"No," I said. "We're all about the same. Six feet is the tallest."

"Guess we'll have to start working on your ball-handling skills, then, won't we?"

"We will?" I asked. "Why is that?"

"Well," Rocket Rod said, "how many six-foot power forwards have you ever seen in high school, let alone college?"

"I don't know," I answered doubtfully. "Not many, I guess."

"Ha ha, you guessed right," Rocket Rod said, extending a bony hand for me to shake.

It was one of those moments that stick with you, stored away and waiting for the time when you're capable of understanding it fully.

For me, that time came the very next season.

I'm a sophomore point guard on a varsity team gutted by desertions among upperclassmen unhappy with Rocket Rod's coaching style. It's the Tournament of Champions, my hometown's showcase event, held every year in front of sold-out crowds at the Civic Center, and I'm bringing the ball up court against pressure. The opposing team's point guard, a senior with quick hands and a low center of gravity, has already sniffed out my weak left hand. He forces me to that side, reaches in, and taps the ball free. Then he's racing to the opposite end of the floor for an uncontested layup.

The scenario plays itself out once, twice, three times, before Rocket Rod is forced to take a time out. "Steady as she goes, son," he says, arm around my shoulder. "This is your team now, and you've to take care of it." I nod and look up at the scoreboard. It's the first quarter, and already we're down by 15 points. The crowd of two thousand sits in stunned silence. This is not what they came to see. They're used to TOC championships, twenty-win seasons, deep runs in the state tournament. Only now are they beginning to realize that those days are over, just as I'm beginning to realize what my fate for the next three seasons will be.

The best player on the worst team in the history of the school.

That, at any rate, was the assessment made by the father of one of my classmates in a barbershop at the tail end of my senior year. I just sat there, trapped in the barber's chair, bib tight around my neck, feeling the red rise up in my face. By then, Rocket Rod was long gone, having been fired after two seasons during which the team won a total of 7 or 8 games while losing something like 34 (the grand total for my three-year varsity career would be 11 wins and 52 losses).

I vividly remember, late in that senior season (a season during

which I wore #44, the same number Pistol Pete had worn while playing for the Atlanta Hawks), a nothing game against a nothing team in
which I would go for 20 points and 10 assists and our team would lose
by 30. By then, there were perhaps eighty people in the stands for our
home games in the Civic Center, more than half that number brought
in on buses by the opposing team. I have a distinct memory of looking
up as I brought the ball up court and seeing my parents sitting there in
the stands, the two of them suffering through yet another Red Demon
loss with grimly stoical looks on their faces. *Why?* I had to ask myself.
*Why do they keep coming to my games when they know beforehand
what the result will be?*

The answer, of course, was that I was their child and they loved me.
I knew that, but in a way it only made matters worse.

*How can something that once gave me such pleasure now cause such
misery?* But even as I thought this, I knew that no good answer would
ever exist.

During a ten-year career in the NBA, mostly spent with the lowly New
Orleans Jazz, Pistol Pete put up some huge numbers (31 points per
game in 1976, his best year in the pros) and made a number of spectacular plays that, in the words of Red Auerbach, defied not just "the
laws of gravity" but "the laws of physics" as well. But all those points
came at a cost. An expansion franchise, the 1974–1975 Jazz won just
4 of its first 38 games. Over the course of the five seasons Pistol Pete
spent with the team, its cumulative record was 161 wins against 249
losses. But, just as had been the case at LSU, winning was largely irrelevant in New Orleans, where everyone understood that seeing Pistol
Pete put on a show was the whole point of the exercise.

And put on a show Pete did. In a game in New York in February 1977, he scorched a Knicks backcourt that included future Hall of
Famers Earl "the Pearl" Monroe and Walt Frazier for 68 points. "His
performance was the best I've ever seen by a guard," said the Knicks
coach, Red Holzman.

Did scoring all those points make Pistol Pete happy?

Unfortunately, no. It only raised expectations. "As morning rolled around the next day," Pete would remember of his record-breaking game, "I wanted nothing more than to stay in bed and hope the world would somehow disappear."

By now, Pistol Pete had come to understand that happiness could not be found inside the lines of a basketball court. And so he began to seek it elsewhere—in booze, first, and then in an unending stream of "isms": vegetarianism, Hinduism, "extraterrestrialism" (the belief that one day a UFO would land on the roof of his apartment and take him away). Meanwhile, the losses piled up like confetti on a parade route. A November 1978 profile of Maravich in *Sports Illustrated* began with the following epigraph from Lou Hudson: "Raw-talent-wise, he's the greatest who ever played. The difference comes down to style. He will be a loser, always, no matter what he does. That's his legacy."

Unfortunately, the last year of Pistol Pete's pro career tends to confirm this idea. Traded to Auerbach's Celtics in the middle of the 1979–1980 season, Pistol Pete, aging and hobbled by knee injuries, suddenly found himself playing backup to another player. He stuck it out in that unfamiliar role for the rest of that season, then retired before the start of the 1980–1981 season, which would end with the Celtics cutting down the nets on another NBA championship. By then, Pete was living as a recluse in New Orleans, rarely leaving home unless it was to stockpile food (he was now in a full-blown survivalist mode) or to drive his Porsche on a Lake Pontchartrain bridge at 150 mph.

"So many times, suicide came into my thoughts," he'd remember. "All I had to do was turn the wheel just ten degrees, and it would be history. Everyone would say, 'What an accident. Isn't it terrible what happened to Pistol Pete?'" But he'd know the truth, and in a sense, that truth would set him free.

According to the German philosopher Ludwig Marcuse, there is no such thing as lasting or eternal happiness. Instead, happiness is a fleeting thing (we feel it briefly, then it fades away). For contemporary happiness researchers like Sonja Lyubomirsky, whatever happiness we might experience in this life is brought about not by a single determining factor but rather by a mix of factors including genetics (50 percent), external living conditions (10 percent), and mental attitude (40 percent). Since the last of these factors, mental attitude, is the only one even remotely under our control, it behooves us, Lyubomirsky suggests, to live our lives in a spirit of gratitude, forgiveness, and optimism. It is only by living in this way—and by choosing work that is meaningful to us—that we can hope to maximize whatever modicum of happiness we are capable of experiencing.

Although a couple of small colleges in Kansas recruited me in a half-assed sort of way, in the end no scholarship offers were ever put on the table, and it's highly doubtful I would've accepted any if they had been. The truth was, by the end of my junior season, when Rocket Rod was fired and a new coach was brought in, I was more or less finished with basketball. I kept on practicing and playing the game, of course, but pretty much all of the passion I'd formerly felt for the sport had evaporated in the course of all those horrific losses.

The summer before my senior year, I surprised everyone (myself included) when I wandered into the high school weight room and declared my intention to play football that fall. "What took you so long?" Coach Masters asked, a smile on his broad face. "Heck, I expected you in here a year ago." That team went something like 6–4 and lost in the second round of the playoffs, but to me it felt like we had won the Super Bowl.

In college at the University of Kansas, I followed the fortunes of the Jayhawks dutifully but at a distance. Certainly I had no illusions about trying out for the team or even playing intramural ball. My passions were focused on other things. I read Hardy and Hemingway, went to Jackson Pollock exhibitions, listened to Coltrane and Monk play "'Round Midnight." I began to write a little, too, albeit in an exploratory sort of way, careful not to dream too extravagantly. In 1986, while studying in England at the University of Essex, I was approached by another student from Kansas who'd tried out for and made a travel team that was being put together for an overseas tour.

"Dude, it's insane," my fellow Kansan said. "They're calling it an English team, but all of the players are from Yugoslavia, Italy, and the United States. You've got to try out."

"I don't think so," I said.

"We're gonna play in *Spain*," the guy said. "We're gonna play in freaking *Israel*."

He couldn't understand how I could pass up the chance to play what he always referred to as "college ball in Europe."

"It's not college ball," I reminded him.

"Well, maybe not," he allowed. "But it's *something*. It's an *opportunity*."

Finally, to get him to stop pestering me, I borrowed a pair of sneakers and went to one of the team's practices. A couple of the Serbian players were really good, and I had some fun throwing alley-oop passes for them to dunk on fast breaks. But even as I was throwing up those passes (shades of "Red on Roundball: Alley-Oop"), another part of me was reliving the pain and disappointment occasioned by all fifty-two of those lopsided high school losses.

They're still right here with me, I thought with amazement. *Probably they'll always be with me. My God, what a waste of human emotion.*

In the years after he retired from the NBA, Pistol Pete ramped up his search for the secret to happiness, arriving finally at a fundamentalist version of his Serbian ancestors' Christian faith. Unable to sleep one night, his mind tortured by flashbacks, regret closing in on him from all sides, Pistol Pete heard God announce in a loud voice, *Be strong and lift thine own heart.* He woke his wife, Jackie, and asked if she'd heard the voice, too, but she just looked at him like he was crazy and told him to go back to sleep.

From that day forward, Pistol Pete read the Bible three or four hours a day, devoting himself to it as he'd once devoted himself to "homework basketball." He visited churches to give his testimony and volunteered at basketball camps so he could bring young campers to Jesus. Against all odds, he became a powerful and effective public speaker, something that those who'd known him in his earlier life couldn't believe. He spoke at high schools, prisons, psych wards, Billy Graham crusades. "He was like a different person," Jackie said. "I saw how happy he was, how he was at peace with everything. I kind of envied him. I wanted that." An old college friend who saw him speak said the same thing. "He was in complete control. For the first time since I'd known him, I thought he was happy."

On January 5, 1988, Pistol Pete was invited to play a pickup basketball game in Pasadena, California. Among those playing in the game was James Dobson, the founder of the evangelical radio program *Focus on the Family*. At the time of the game, Pete hadn't picked up a basketball in months, but Dobson, an intense man and something of a basketball fanatic, pressed him to play.

The game was four-on-four, and on Dobson's team was a seven-foot fellow evangelist named Ralph Drollinger who'd played on John Wooden's last NCAA championship team at UCLA. During a break in the action, Dobson and Pistol Pete were shooting three pointers while Drollinger rebounded.

"Two weeks ago, I couldn't even get my arm up this high," Pete confessed to Dobson, raising his right arm over his head, hand in the cookie jar.

"How do you feel now?" Dobson asked.

"I feel great," Pete said.

Moments later, he dropped dead, right there on the floor of the gymnasium.

I was walking across Mount Oread on the KU campus when I heard the news. It was in the early days of the 1987–1988 season, when the

Jayhawks, led by senior Danny Manning and coach Larry Brown, won an NCAA title in Kansas City. A former teammate from Dodge City ran up to me on the sidewalk in front of Watson Library. "Did you hear?" he asked, out of breath. "Pistol Pete's dead. Keeled over playing hoops, barely forty years old."

"What was it?" I asked. "Heart attack?"

"That's what they're saying."

We stood there together a moment longer, then my teammate continued on to his class in Wescoe, and I continued on to mine in Fraser Hall, where the subject of the day was existentialism and the imperative each of us lives under to discover meaning, however fleeting, in these lives we've been given.

Did Pistol Pete die happy? I wondered. Did he raise his eyes a final time before his heart stopped beating? What did he see up there? The face of God? Press Maravich's expectant scowl? An empty ring that could never be filled, no matter how many basketballs were made to pass through it?

It's a question that only God or Pistol Pete himself could answer.

—7—
Biscuits and Meth

I no longer recall what compelled me to drive out to the Gunsmoke Truck Stop that Sunday afternoon in May, but it couldn't have been my need of a job. I'd been driving a four-wheel-drive tractor and babysitting recalcitrant irrigation equipment on my father's wheat farm for six summers running, and the same job was waiting for me if I wanted it. But maybe that sameness was the problem. Maybe at that point in my life—the summer between my junior and senior years of high school—I was in need of a change, a break in the monotonous pattern my life had fallen into: conditioning in the fall, basketball in the winter, working on the farm all spring and summer. Maybe, without thinking it all through, I'd decided to break out into the wider world about which, at that point, I still knew so little.

The Gunsmoke sat on a wide gravel lot just off Highway 283 on the southern edge of Dodge City. Just to the north was Maupin Truck Parts with its "largest inventory of new and used truck parts between Kansas City and Denver," while to the south there opened a lonesome stretch of highway that had been built more or less on top of the old Western Trail used by cattle drovers bringing herds north from Texas in the 1870s and 1880s. By no stretch of the imagination was this a busy part of town. The Hitchin' Post Truck Stop, on East Wyatt Earp Boulevard, saw far more traffic in both cars and trucks. By comparison, the Gunsmoke had a sleepy, rural feel. Its stock-in-trade was not midnight travelers or cross-country haulers (unlike the Hitchin' Post, which was open twenty-four hours a day, the Gunsmoke closed at 10 p.m.), but rather the small army of cattle trucks ("bull haulers") and refrigerated trucks ("reefers") that serviced the area's feedlots and beef packing plants.

On the Sunday I showed up, the place had the aura of an Old West ghost town. Dust devils swirled in the gravel lot, where a few tractor-trailers sat idling. Only a half dozen or so flatbed ranch trucks filled the parking spaces in front of the restaurant, a brown metal building with the word G U N S M O K E mounted on the roof in big white letters someone had cut from plywood with a jigsaw. I remember thinking, *I've wasted a trip. There can't possibly be any work here, and even if there is, whoever does the hiring is going to be at home taking a nap about now.*

Nevertheless, I pushed through the front doors of the restaurant and asked the woman at the hostess station where I could find the manager.

"Which one?" the hostess asked, yawning. "Restaurant or filling station?"

"Filling station," I answered, for it had never occurred to me to apply for a job in a restaurant.

"That'd be Merv," she said. "Head down the sidewalk on the north side of the building, and you'll find him in his office. If you hear snoring, just cough or clear your throat. That's what I do."

The wind kicked up sand all around me as I made my way down the walk to a second set of glass doors, through which I found an unmanned cash register, a couple of large arcade games (Pac Man, Donkey Kong), and a bank of pay phones with a couple of rickety wooden tables set before them. At the back of the room, halfway between the phones and the register, a partially closed door led to a small office from inside of which came a groggy voice. "Hello? Can I help you?"

"Yes, I came to ask about a job."

At this, the door to the office was pulled open from within, revealing a crumbled-looking man with a brown, leathery face and striking pale blue eyes. "A job, huh? Well, I wish I could offer you a job. Business has been terrible slow of late."

"That's okay," I said, turning to go.

"What's your name?" the man asked, holding me there with his eyes. "You look familiar."

I told him, adding, "You probably know my dad."

"Harold or Bill?" he asked.

"Bill."

"Well, sure, I know Bill," he said, using the heels of his cowboy boots to wheel his chair out of the office far enough to shake my hand. "Mervin Sinclair."

"Good to meet you."

He fixed me again with his pale blue eyes. "Why aren't you working for your old man? You two didn't have a falling out, did you?"

"No," I said. "Nothing like that."

"Well, good. One thing I've learned in this life. There ain't nothing more important than family. You still in school?"

"Yeah, for another month."

"What else you got going on? Are you running track? Playing baseball?"

"No, just school," I said.

I was wondering why we were even having this conversation when the man rolled back into his office and moved some coats and a stack of shop rags from a large Naugahyde couch. "Come in and have a seat. I was just getting caught up on the papers. What do you read, the *Wichita Eagle* or the *Hutchinson News?*"

"The *Eagle*," I said, although in truth I read neither.

"Here you go, then," he said, handing me a fat stack of newsprint.

I sat down on the too-soft couch and began reading the sports section. Meanwhile, Merv leaned back in his swivel chair and put his booted feet on the desk, the sports section of the Hutch paper open before him. Every once in a while he'd grunt or shake his head. Otherwise all was quiet but for the rustling of newsprint.

"Ready to trade?" he asked after ten minutes or so.

"Sure."

We traded sports sections, and silence descended for another ten or fifteen minutes. Then, yawning and pretending to consult my watch, I rose and said I'd better get going.

"All right," Merv said without looking up from his paper. "What time does school let out these days?"

"Two forty-five."

"How long do you think it would take you to get from there to here?"

"I don't know. Fifteen or twenty minutes."

"Fine," he said. "See you tomorrow around three o'clock?"

And so it began.

The job paid $5.50 an hour—two dollars above the minimum wage—plus "all the biscuits and gravy you can eat." It's hard to say which part of the deal was sweeter. With so little time to spend it, the pile of money I took home each week just grew and grew. After a while, I had so much put away that I forgot to deposit the weekly checks, and the bookkeeper had to come over from the restaurant and lay into me about it. Then there were the biscuits, which were flaky on the outside and melt-in-your-mouth soft on the inside and covered from one end of the plate to the other with thick sausage gravy. "Just like Mama used to make," the menu bragged, and although my mother was more of the Bran Flakes-and-fruit type, I got the point all the same. For the bull haulers and reefer drivers who frequented the Gunsmoke, biscuits and gravy was a fragrant, high-calorie reminder of the homes they saw so infrequently.

Almost as good as the money and free biscuits was the endless stream of interesting characters who populated the truck stop: tire men and waitresses, cooks and dishwashers, custom cutters, oil exploration crews, farmers and cattle ranchers, the guys from Maupin Truck Parts. To my young eyes, used to monotonous rolling pastures and wheat fields devoid of people, the cast of characters was fascinating and strange. There was the 300-pound bus boy, son of one of the janitors, who could play Donkey Kong for hours on a single fifty-cent credit, fueled by nothing but cinnamon rolls and Mountain Dew.

There was the seventy-year-old waitress whose battered station wagon was so full of old newspapers and clothes that it was impossible to see in any of the car's windows except the front windshield and the driver's side door. There was the owner of the local Cadillac dealership, who liked to boast that in ten years of coming to breakfast at the Gunsmoke he'd "never driven the same car twice," and the thirty-something prostitute who insisted, no matter how many times she was caught plying her trade, that she was "just a broke college kid looking for a ride back home."

Everyone had a story to tell or seemed to be acting out a part in the wider drama. Merv, for example, was the henpecked former truck driver who had been "grounded" after a long career on the road by "The Queen Bee," his redheaded wife of forty years, who ran the restaurant side of the business with a stern authority that was the exact opposite of Merv's laidback approach. Whenever they fought, which happened at least once a week, every part of the exchange was carried out in public and included an extensive cast of bit players and extras. A waitress would show up at the filling station and announce to Merv (and anyone else who happened to be there at the time) that The Queen Bee wanted to talk to him over at the restaurant right away. There were certain "issues" they needed to discuss.

"Issues," Merv would mutter from behind his newspaper. "Is that her word or yours?"

"Hers."

"Well, you can go back over there and tell her I'm just a *little* too busy right now."

All this was not said so much as acted out for the benefit of anyone who might be listening.

Even we lowly tire men and diesel jocks had our roles to play. There was Gavin, the skinny, bespectacled junior college student who showed me how to pump diesel and fix flats and whose mother was a war bride from Germany who professed not to understand "deese Americain cheeeeldren wit deeer drugs und what-have-you." Or Monty, the chain-smoking, acne-scarred tire man who'd dropped out of high school after knocking up his fifteen-year-old girlfriend, and who now worked a "daily double," pumping diesel and fixing flats from 6 a.m. to 3 p.m., and working as a short order cook in the restaurant from 6 p.m. until almost 11. As for me, I was the "new guy," often the "fucking new guy," an athlete from a farm family who'd taken a job at the truck stop for reasons that were not at all satisfactory or clear. "He's a goddamn *football* player, for Christsake," I overheard Monty saying to Gavin shortly after I was hired. "What the hell is a football player doing working here? I fucking hate football players, and now we've got one working *here,* at the Gunsmoke?"

However, all of these people were mere bit players compared with the true stars of the place. Truck drivers may have occupied a lowly position in society as a whole, but in the world of the Gunsmoke, they were kings. Everything we did, and most everything that happened at the Gunsmoke, revolved around them.

There were rich truckers (the kind who owned their own rigs) and poor truckers, fat truckers and skinny truckers, young truckers and old truckers, male truckers and female truckers (albeit far fewer of the latter), white truckers and black truckers, dirty truckers and fastidiously clean truckers, born-again truckers and wildly blasphemous truckers, cowboy truckers and those who preferred tracksuits and sneakers, illiterate truckers and those with master's degrees and even PhDs. . . . And yet, for all of these outward differences, most of the truckers I came to know shared a remarkably consistent vision. When asked why they'd chosen the trucking life, with its public showers, artery-clogging food, and long periods away from home, they'd all say, "I gotta be free" or "I'm not fit for a regular job" or "I don't know—just lazy, I guess." To a man, they thought of themselves as misfits and rebels. What they did was not work. It was more of a calling or a lifestyle, like being a biker or a cowboy or a country singer. Indeed, from what I could see, most didn't think of themselves as truckers at all but rather as free spirits who just happened to drive trucks.

Yet for all their rebel talk, most of the truckers I met at the Gunsmoke were slaves to one thing or another. A clock was always ticking

somewhere nearby; there was always someplace else they were supposed to be—if not right at that moment, then *soon soon soon.*

"They're expecting me at the feedlot right now."

"Supposed to be in Dallas by morning. Think I'll make it?"

"Gotta be in Sacramento Friday night and in New York four days
later."

The pressure to make these deadlines was enormous, and the obstacles standing in the way were many. Miles. Road construction. Un-
ruly animals. Weather. Flat tires and other mechanical failures. The
speed limit. The max-weight limit. The difficult math of keeping a
logbook with at least some resemblance to reality. The need to eat, to
shower, to sleep. Different drivers dealt with the pressure in different
ways, but from what I could see, they all felt it, most of them intensely.

Although we saw our share of long-haul reefer drivers, the ma-
jority of the truckers who frequented the Gunsmoke were bull haulers—short- to middle-distance truckers who delivered live cattle from
feedlots across the southern plains to the packing plants east of town.
In theory, bull haulers worked regular hours and slept in their own
beds far more often than reefer drivers did. However, in my experience, this difference was mostly an illusion. Driving twenty hours
straight was the same fate whether you crossed four states or never left
the same four counties of Kansas. Either way, you had to stay awake
and arrive where you were supposed to be on time. Both kinds of drivers "cooked" their logbooks, broke the speed and max-weight limits
with impunity, and regularly ingested any and all drugs they could
lay their hands on: caffeine, tobacco, alcohol, prescription pain kill-
ers, marijuana, speed, cocaine, and, perhaps most of all, a brownish,
powdery substance they called "crank" but that nowadays goes by the
name methamphetamine, "meth" for short.

I came into this knowledge gradually. When I first started working at the Gunsmoke, it was Gavin the drivers knew and trusted, not
me. I remember one day we were fixing a flat on a trailer belonging
to a bull hauler we called "Duvall" because he looked like the actor
Robert Duvall. Halfway through the job, as I was waiting for the patch

glue to dry, I saw Gavin and Duvall disappear into the cab of Duvall's Freightliner. Soon Hank Williams's "Long Gone Lonesome Blues" was blaring from the cab, and when they emerged, five minutes later, they were accompanied by a great, billowing cloud of marijuana smoke of the kind you might see in a Cheech & Chong movie, both of them laughing and horsing around.

I was stunned. It was not the fact that Gavin had gotten high at work or that a truck driver who was about to haul a large and dangerous load had done the same. No, it was the *kind* of driver combined with the *kind* of drug that shocked me, for in my mind, men like Duvall—early fifties, crewcut under cowboy hat, wire-rim bifocals, starched pearl-button shirt—didn't smoke pot. Instead, they delivered lectures, often as part of a church or Boy Scout meeting, about marijuana being a "gateway drug." And yet here my own eyes and ears were telling me that that wasn't necessarily true, at least not at the Gunsmoke. When Duvall drove off that day, and I asked Gavin about it, he just shrugged and gave me a cockeyed smile.

"Shit, all these drivers are potheads, even the ones that look like your grandpa. It takes the edge off all the crank they do."

Exhibit A in this regard was a man I'll call Johnny Mac. He was a legendary figure at the Gunsmoke, a bull hauler who was also an OCD-grade clean freak. "Goddamn, you could fucking eat off the floor of that boy's cattle wagon," his fellow bull haulers would marvel when they saw his rig. "How in the hell does he keep it so goddamn clean?" To which the only appropriate answer was a bemused shrugging of the shoulders.

Though tall at six foot two and fat in the way of NFL linemen, Johnny Mac also possessed exceedingly small feet and hands, an anomaly he drew attention to by wearing $1,000 ostrich skin boots and making sure that his fingernails were always manicured. But even this was only a small part of the Johnny Mac legend. For on top of everything else, the man was a notorious crank addict. He kept an engraved silver vial of the stuff in his breast pocket at all times, and he liked to pull it out in front of anyone who might be lounging about the station and slowly tap tap tap the brownish powder into an open can of Dr. Pepper, which he always referred to as "Dr. Pecker." That done, he'd stir the concoction with a swizzle stick, toss off a hearty laugh, and drink it down in a series of long gulps, followed by a lip-smacking smile of satisfaction.

Whenever this happened, Gavin would be sure to disappear into the tire shop or through the metal door leading to the kitchen. When I called him out on this odd behavior, he turned white as a sheet, then related how he'd once done a "Dr. Pecker" with Johnny Mac, and the result had been twenty-four hours of sleepless terror during which he'd feared that his heart would explode.

"Now every time that fat son of a bitch comes in, he wants me to do it all over again. Can you believe that shit? Calls me a pussy when I won't do it. Fucking crazy!"

Not all drivers were like Johnny Mac, of course. One in particular stands out in my memory as a kind of anti-Mac—or at least that's the way I saw him at the time. His name was Earl, and he was the owner-operator of a sparkling new Freightliner conventional with aluminum wheels and a customized, double-wide sleeper. He owned a second truck, too, almost as nice, which he hired another man to drive for him. But the defining part of Earl's character, at least as I saw it, was the fact that he didn't drink or take drugs.

"Those days are behind me, thank the Lord," he'd say, lighting a fresh Pall Mall from the embers of the one he'd just finished smoking. "At one time, I was as bad as any of these jokers you see around here—worse, probably. I had pills I took to sleep, pills I took to wake up, and a third kind of pills I took to regulate any disputes that arose between the first two. Add that to the two liters of Smirnoff I poured down my throat each and every day, and I guess you could say I was one of them 'chemical people' Mrs. Reagan is always talking about."

A reefer driver, Earl spent a lot of time waiting for one or both of his trailers to be loaded at the beef plant, and he liked to spend this down time smoking and drinking coffee in the filling station. We often shared a table on slow Saturday nights or Sunday mornings, me catching up on my homework, Earl reliving the biggest successes and disappointments he'd experienced in almost forty years of "going down the road." As a result, I soon knew more about the basic contours of Earl's life and his views on the world than I knew about members of my own family.

"I come from nothing, son, just your everyday, run-of-the-mill Oklahoma sharecroppers," he liked to say, his brown eyes spectacularly bloodshot, his long face a mass of loose wrinkles like a bloodhound's face. "My daddy drank himself to death before the age of fifty, same as his daddy and all his brothers, and I was well on the way to joining them when I quit."

"How did you do it?" I'd ask.

"Same as Johnny Cash. Got religion. Believe me, if there'd been any other road, I'd have taken it, but there wasn't then, and there still ain't now. Trust me, son. Old Earl knows all about Jesus and the devil both."

Earl's view of other truck drivers was that they were stubborn, stupid, and headed straight to hell, and yet he had great affection for them, too. If he and Johnny Mac crossed paths, for example, as sometimes happened, he'd joke around with him, maybe ribbing him about his weight. "John, I swear, if you get any fatter you're gonna need a mirror just to see your own pecker." Only when Johnny Mac was gone would he shake his head and say, "My God, what a train wreck!"

With me, however, he was always curiously deferential. "Son, you're on the right track," he'd say, nodding at the books I had spread out before me. "You know how old I was when I quit school?"

"No, Earl. How old?"

"Fourteen. Can you guess why I quit at that particular age?"

"Let's see. Got your driver's license?"

"Ha! Little genius, ain't you? What grade you in?"

"Senior in high school."

"You a drinker?"

"Some."

"Do any drugs?"

"Not really. Just some pot when it's offered and I'm in the mood for it."

"Uh huh. You're what's called a recreational user. For me, it was always more like a full-time job. Eighty, ninety, a hundred hours a week. It got to a point where I didn't wanna live no more. Figured one of these days I'd just pick out some loser barreling down from the opposite direction and put us both out of our misery."

The idea of a whacked-out trucker committing suicide by crossing the centerline was something of an urban legend at the Gunsmoke. I'd heard the stories more times than I could remember, just never with the absolute seriousness Earl gave the subject.

"Well then, why didn't you?"

Here the man shrugged and lit another Pall Mall.

"Who knows? The hand of God just kinda reached out and stopped me, I guess."

One night, six or seven months after I started at the truck stop, I was offered a closer look at that whole "world of the road" Earl was always talking about. It was around nine o'clock on a Saturday night, and I'd just finished fixing a trailer tire for a young bull hauler I'll call Donny. As I was writing up his ticket, Donny, who was in his late twenties and sported shoulder-length blond hair beneath a straw cowboy hat, emerged from the men's room and did an unsteady jig on the station floor. "Whooeee, I gotta pick up a load of fats over at Liberal in two hours and I am already soooooooo fucked up."

"I can see that," I said.

"Say, why don't you come along with me?" he asked out of the blue. "Hell, yes! You're getting off soon, right?"

"In about an hour," I said, very noncommittal.

"Perfect!" Donny said.

I'd been to Liberal many times to play football and basketball. It was a flat, dirty town with even less to recommend it than Dodge City.

"Thanks," I said. "I think I'll pass."

"Oh, come on," Donny said. "Be a friend. I've been up for two days straight, and this is my last load of the night. Fucking Gavin would do it! Hell, yeah! Gavin's taken plenty of rides with me!"

An hour later, I found myself climbing into the passenger seat of Donny's ten-year-old cabover Pete. "That's it, that's it, get on up here," Donny said. "Just take that stuff at your feet and toss it into the sleeper."

The truck's interior was upholstered in red Naugahyde held together in places by strips of gray duct tape. Dirty clothes, porn magazines, empty Coke bottles, and crumpled cigarette packages littered the floor. Despite the dozen or so wintergreen air fresheners dangling from the passenger-side sun visor, the truck smelled strongly of sweat, beer, cigarettes, and marijuana.

"Reach in the glove box and bring out Walt, if you don't mind," Donny said as we wheeled out of the lot and headed south on Highway 283. "Walt" turned out to be a well-seasoned meerschaum pipe with the head of Sir Walter Raleigh carved into its bowl. It was already loaded to the brim with weed.

"You smoke pot out of this thing?" I asked.

"Why, yes I do," Donny said. "Now fire it up, why don't you."

I did as I was told, and soon we were flying down the southbound highway singing along to Neil Young's *Harvest* album. *Old man take a look at my life. I'm a lot like you. I need someone to love me the whole day through.* We passed through the Big Basin near St. Jacob's Well, rolling ranch country with virtually no one on the road but us. We'd not gone twenty miles when Donny pulled over at a gas station in Minneola, emerging a minute later with a fresh pack of Marlboros and a couple of quart bottles of Miller High Life. "Here you go," Donny said, handing me a bottle. "Little something to wet your whistle." By the town of Meade, where we stopped to take a leak and where Donny loaded up on four more quarts of High Life, I was having trouble forming coherent sentences. I'd start saying something, but then the point of it would become lost on me, and I'd have to pause or start over.

"What are you, some kind of lightweight?" Donny laughed. "This isn't even my party dope. This is just my on-the-job dope."

"Well, okay, but . . . uh. . . ."

"Lord Almighty," Donny said, shaking his head.

An hour later, we pulled into a line of trucks on a sand road with deep ditches on either side. In the distance, perhaps an eighth of a mile away, I could see the floodlit hardpan of a feedlot—pen after pen of fat cattle with a feed mill rising up in the background like a sky-scraper. Every time the trucks in front of us in line rolled forward, we followed suit. Meanwhile, Donny did two lines of crank off the glossy cover of a porn magazine and shoved AC/DC's *Back in Black* into the cassette player. The ominous opening of "Hells Bells" filled the cab.

"Reach for Walter, if you would."

"Donny . . . I. . . ."

"Don't worry, boy. I ain't gonna ask you to *talk* or anything. Ha ha ha!"

When our turn to be loaded arrived, Donny expertly backed the truck up to the concrete ramp and put on galoshes and a pair of coveralls he kept stowed away in a side compartment of his aluminum trailer. I stayed in the truck, watching in the rearview mirror as Donny and another man pushed fifty or so fat cattle up a shit-covered aluminum ramp and into topside compartments of the double-decker trailer. The cab of the Peterbilt rocked back and forth on its baffled shock absorbers like a boat in high seas. That was 50,000 pounds of prime US beef they were loading back there. It was a live and moving thing, a bawling, breathing, kicking, pissing, shitting thing that could break a man's arm or blow his knee out with a single slip or kick. And back there among them, sliding around on shit-coated galoshes, half-drunk and stoned out of his mind, was good old Donny. *So this is the great American trucker at work,* I thought. *God help us all.*

After the truck was loaded and weighed, and Donny had stowed away his galoshes and coveralls, we started back down the road to Dodge. "Hell, it ain't even twelve-thirty, and we're already loaded and headed home," Donny rejoiced. "We'll have these doggies dropped off by two-thirty, the truck put away by three. After that, it's party time! Yeah, baby!"

Stopping once again in Meade, Donny bought two large cherry Cokes in Styrofoam cups and split a pint of Jack Daniels between them. By the time we hit the outskirts of Dodge, I was as drunk and stoned as I'd ever been in my life. "Hell, don't you high school kids *party* anymore?" Donny asked. "Shit, when I was your age, we used to drink a half pint of Jack before *first period,* and here you can't even hold up your end of a Saturday night. What's the world coming to, anyhow?"

Rather than taking me on the last part of his run, he dropped me off behind the Gunsmoke, where I spent a half hour vomiting between two trash dumpsters before crawling into the back of my Firebird and passing out. When I awoke, around eight the next morning, I was already two hours late for work.

"Well, well, well, will you look at what the cat dragged in," Merv observed from behind his Sunday paper. "So tell me, how was Liberal?"

"You know about that?" I asked, feeling like I might start throwing up all over again right there on the station floor.

"Of course I do," Merv said. "Donny was in for biscuits and gravy two hours ago, and didn't he have a tale to tell."

That's the way it always was at the truck stop. First the deed, then the dramatic reenactment.

In the fall of my second year at the truck stop, Gavin left for college in Wichita, and in a single stroke I went from being "the fucking new guy" to being, after Monty, the most experienced hand at the Gunsmoke. The sports I'd played in high school were a thing of the past now. As Gavin had done, I attended classes at the community college weekday mornings from eight until noon. Afternoons, evenings, and weekends I spent at the Gunsmoke. Counting overtime, I was grossing something like four hundred dollars a week, of which I managed to spend perhaps twenty. It was a very sweet deal, and, like Gavin, I probably would've continued working there all the way through my sophomore year of college had something not happened to destroy the detached, ironical lens through which I viewed the place and its inhabitants.

Sunday morning was my favorite time at the Gunsmoke. There was no business to speak of, and usually I'd knocked out all of my school-work the day before, leaving me nothing to do but lounge around the office reading the Sunday papers with Merv. We had a well-established Sunday morning routine. I'd sneak into the station around 6:15 or 6:30, careful not to wake Merv where he dozed in the office, then slip over to the kitchen to get us a pot of coffee and a couple of giant cinnamon rolls.

However, on this particular Sunday, the whole routine was off. Instead of sleeping in his office, Merv was sitting at one of the rick-ety tables beneath the bank of pay phones, all of the station lights switched off, staring out the front windows at the trucks lined up in the gravel lot.

"What's going on?" I asked, stopping short just inside the door.

"Oh, that's right," Merv said. "You don't know."

"Know what?"

"Earl," Merv said ominously.

"What about him?"

"Last night, after you went home, he came storming into the res-taurant and threw up all over the dining room floor. Monty and I had to drag his sorry ass out of there, and what do you know, he threw up over here, too. Right about where you're standing."

I looked down at the dirty red tiles at my feet, still not getting it.

"He threw up? Wait a minute. Are you telling me—"

Merv nodded slowly, eyes half-closed. "That's right," he said, point-ing out the window at where Earl's Freightliner idled in the darkness. "I don't know when or why the sumbitch fell off the wagon, but by the time he rolled in here last night, he was already drunker than shit."

It took a moment for all of this to sink in. Unlike Merv, I'd never met "Bad Earl," only "Good Earl" with his tales of Johnny Cash–style redemption.

"What's he doing now?" I asked. "Sleeping it off?"

"Ha!" Merv laughed. "Guys like Earl don't *sleep it off*. They pass out for a while, but when they wake up, they go right back to it, full-tilt and balls-to-the-wall. Give him an hour, and he'll be in here raising hell all over again."

At this, we both looked out across the gravel lot at where Earl's truck stood idling. *He's in there*, I thought. *Earl. Drunk off his ass.*

"What do you think brought it on?" I asked.

"Shit, who knows?" Merv said. "Could've been almost anything. Most of the time, these guys don't even need a reason."

There was something about Merv's tone that bothered me. It was like Earl had ceased to be the flesh-and-blood man we knew and had morphed into something sinister and strange, an outsider to be shunned rather than a member of the extended truck stop family who deserved our pity and understanding.

Around eight o'clock that morning, Merv managed to get Earl's wife on the phone. There was a lot of "Yes, ma'am" and "No, ma'am" and "I'm sorry to have to be the one to tell you, ma'am," as he ran down the situation, but what it finally boiled down to was Merv making a promise we'd keep Earl at the Gunsmoke until she had time to find a replacement driver for Earl's load and make her way up from Oklahoma City to collect him. The trip was five hours, give or take.

"Five hours!" Merv said, after he'd hung up. "We're supposed to babysit that lunatic for five hours?"

We sat around talking about it between ourselves as well as with various Sunday morning regulars who drifted over from the restaurant, where the "situation with Earl" was a topic of hot debate. There were those who believed that Merv had had no right to call Earl's wife and that by doing so he'd violated some unwritten part of the trucker's code. Others believed just as strongly that Merv was in the right. After all, there was a load of beef sitting on Earl's truck even as we spoke, and someone somewhere in America was expecting that beef to be delivered. Still others ignored this part of the question altogether and focused on what should be done *now*, while we waited for Earl's wife to make her way north from Oklahoma.

"If it were me," said one long-haul driver, "I'd grab a bottle of booze and take it out to Earl's truck as an early Christmas present. The sooner he passes out again, the better off we're all gonna be."

"To heck with booze," an old rancher laughed in response. "How about I run home and get my tranquilizer gun? The second that old boy tries to climb down from his rig, *thunk,* shoot one of them darts right in his ass, ha ha ha."

I couldn't believe what I was hearing. Is this how they treated a fellow member of the hallowed truck stop family? By telling jokes and laughing? By threatening to shoot him in the ass with a tranquilizer gun? Evidently it was.

Finally, though, the chorus grew tired of repeating itself and headed back to the restaurant where an entirely new audience—the after-church crowd—awaited them.

A little later, Merv joined them, too, leaving me with strict instructions to call over to the restaurant should I witness any movement in Earl's Freightliner.

And so it happened that I was by myself when, around ten o'clock that morning, Earl stumbled into the station from the tire shop. How he'd gotten back there—or out of his truck without my noticing—I have no idea.

"Earl," I said.

He stopped where he was, weaving slightly, his hooded, bloodshot eyes empty of recognition. His gray-brown hair, which normally would've been slicked back and covered by a cowboy hat, was plastered flat on one side of his head with what I guessed was dried vomit.

"Earl," I said again, louder.

This time his eyes changed slightly, lighting up for a second before his eyebrows came down and they darkened again. "What you looking at, boy?" he asked, slurring the words so badly that it came out sounding more like "Whuuurrrloooookisshhinglya, baaaaa?"

I could think of nothing to say, and a moment later he wheeled to his left and disappeared into the men's room, where I could hear him puking over and over again. When he emerged a few minutes later, he was angry and incoherent, ranting and raving about matters that made no sense at all.

"Goddamn sumbitch, I fucking *told her*. . . . Nah, nah, nah, *course* not. . . . Blames *me*, same as always. . . ."

He stumbled over to the bank of pay phones as if he'd make a call, then decided against it and fell into a chair at one of the rickety tables by the window, the same chair he'd sat in on so many other Sunday mornings, sipping coffee out of a thermos and smoking one Pall Mall after another while I read the paper or did my homework.

"Your wife's on her way up," I said. "Merv called her."

Earl just looked at me out of those terrible hooded eyes of his.

"What you got to drink in here?" he asked, but again it sounded more like "Whaaaasshhaagoturrdrinnnkkinnneerr?"

"Nothing," I said. "It's Sunday."

This was a lie. Although not a drinker himself, Merv kept a bottle of Seagram's gin in a desk drawer in his office. The stuff tasted like aftershave, which is why none of us tire men and diesel jocks had gotten into it. However, as soon as the thought of that nearly full bottle entered my head, it seemed to enter Earl's, too, through some kind of telepathy. Smiling faintly, he began to push himself up out of his chair. "Have me some of the boss man's stash," he said.

"You've had enough," I said. "Let me get you some coffee instead."

"Coffee!" he exploded. "You wanna give me coffee! Nah, boy. Have me some of that *boss* man's liquor!"

Although Earl outweighed me by forty or fifty pounds, I wasn't particularly worried. He was old and so drunk he could barely stand in his cowboy boots, whereas I was young and athletic and stone-cold sober.

"Sit down," I said firmly.

"Ha!" Earl laughed. "Who's gonna make me? *You?*"

"Damn right," I said, my voice loud in my ears.

But instead of coming at me "full-tilt and balls-to-the-wall," as Merv might have said, Earl just collapsed back into his chair and began to sob. "Oh Lordy, Lordy, Lordy. Somebody give me a goddamn drink already!"

A moment later, the door to the tire shop opened behind me, and I turned to see Merv standing there with a plate of biscuits and gravy in his hand.

"What's he bellyaching about?" he asked.

"He wants that bottle of gin from your desk."

"Well," Merv said, setting the biscuits on the counter. "What are you waiting for? Give it to him."

"Really?"

"Go on," he said, blue eyes drilling into me. "Earl's a grown man."

I looked back and forth between the two men, both of whom had been father figures to me during my time at the Gunsmoke. Although I didn't know it yet, I was done with both of them—and with the truck stop, too.

Shaking my head, I walked into Merv's office, pulled the nearly full bottle of Seagram's from the desk drawer, and carried it to where Earl sat waiting at the wobbly little table. "There," I said, unscrewing the cap and setting the bottle before him. "Have at it."

That he did, grabbing the bottle in both hands and drinking off half of it before pausing to wipe his mouth on his shirt sleeve.

"Think you got it all figured out, doncha?"

"No," I said.

"Sure you do," he said. "Fucking college boy!"

And with that, he upended the bottle again, little trickles of gin spilling down both sides of his face and collecting in the collar of his pearl-button shirt.

When the bottle was empty, Merv and I stood there on the tile floor of the station, watching as the liquor stole into Earl's bloodstream. It didn't take long. Maybe ten minutes after draining the bottle, he lay his head on the table, and a few minutes after that, he began to snore loudly.

"Come on," Merv said. "Let's get him back to his rig before he starts throwing up again."

Together we managed to half-walk, half-drag Earl back to the cab of his idling Freightliner, where a couple of other truckers helped us put him to bed in the sleeper. I remember he had a photograph of his family taped to the mirror above the truck's tiny sink. They were standing in the parking lot of some vast megachurch on the Oklahoma plains, a stiff prairie wind ripping through their hair and clothes. *So he has a daughter,* I thought, wondering why he'd never talked about her—and why I had never asked.

Later that morning, Earl's wife and a man in a denim jacket rolled into the parking lot in a powder blue Cadillac, and Earl was handed down from his truck like Jesus descending from the cross. I stood there watching along with everyone else as his boots were pulled off and he was put to bed on a blanket in the Cadillac's back seat. Before he'd even been properly tucked in, the man in the denim jacket was already wheeling Earl's Freightliner out of the gravel lot, bound for wherever his load was supposed to be at that hour.

"All right," Merv said to the assembled crowd of waitresses and ranch hands and sleep-deprived drivers. "Show's over."

Amen to that, I thought.

A few minutes later, the crowd mostly gone, Merv slapped me on the shoulders as if to say, "Good job, son," and headed back over to the restaurant.

I was alone for the first time since Earl stumbled in from the tire shop. Something inside me had changed while I wasn't paying attention. I could feel it even if I couldn't yet put a name to it.

Passing through the heavy glass door to the station, the first thing I saw was that plate of three-hours-old biscuits and gravy congealing on the counter. I nearly gagged just looking at it, and to this day I've never been able to stomach so much as a bite of the stuff.

—8—

Farewell, My Lovely

I see on the website Classiccars.com that it's still possible to buy a 1970 Firebird Formula 400 in the exact shade of green I knew at the age of seventeen and eighteen, but I'm not deceived. The great days have faded; the end is in sight.

The Formula 400 was the miracle GM had wrought, the sort of machine that came into a person's life perhaps once in a lifetime—and maybe not that often. To truly appreciate its near-mystical beauty and power, you had to be in your late teens, at most your early twenties. True, you could always acquire the car later, as part of some well-funded midlife crisis (the completely restored "ghost green" Formula 400 on Classiccars.com will set you back a mere $64,000), but doing so would make a mockery of what a car like that is really meant to stand for, which is youth with all its gaudy, irretrievable excitements.

My father bought the 400, wrecked, off a dealer's lot in south Dodge City in the fall of 1978. He didn't buy it for himself, but rather as part of an elaborate ploy to coax my eighteen-year-old brother Steve back from a Catholic boarding school in Hays, where he'd absconded the year before to pursue a vague notion of becoming a priest. As it happened, my father owed a certain debt of gratitude to the Catholic Church (as a Depression-era orphan, he'd been adopted through one of its benevolent agencies), and so, in theory, it could have been argued that he should have allowed at least one of his seven sons to join the priesthood. But evidently that's not how he saw the matter, because when Steve began to waver in his commitment after a football injury derailed his senior year, there was Dad dangling the ghost green 400.

"Come on home, son," the car seemed to say in its throaty voice. "There are excitements of a secular sort yet to be had in this life."

A few years later, with Steve safely enrolled as a business major at the University of Kansas, the car came to me. I'd like to pay it the tribute of the sigh that is not a sob.

The Firebird Formula 400 was distinguished from all other makes and models of cars by the fact that a white Trans Am version of it appeared in the 1974 cult classic *Thunderbolt and Lightfoot* starring Jeff Bridges and Clint Eastwood. In the movie's opening sequence, a young drifter (Bridges) steals the car off a lot somewhere on the high plains of Montana. In the joyride that follows, Bridges crosses paths with a bank robber disguised as a preacher (Eastwood) who is on the run from members of his former gang. The two join up, and many wonderful car chases ensue, including one truly bizarre scene involving a 1973 Plymouth Fury driven by a shotgun-toting Child of God with a caged raccoon on the seat beside him. (The entire wonderful sequence is on YouTube. Look it up.)

A more refined cousin of the Chevy Camaro, the Firebird Formula 400 was long, low, and wide, like an alley cat crouching in anticipation of prey. Unlike the three model years that preceded it (1967–1969), which featured four somewhat clunky side windows, the 1970 Firebird had just two, one on each side, to go along with its semi-fastback rear window. The doors through which one gained entrance to the car were heavy and almost impossibly long, threatening the integrity of door handles and hinges every time someone got in or out. (As a practical matter, the 1970 Firebird probably should have had no doors at all, but been entered instead by climbing through the window in the manner of a race driver. That's how I got in and out of mine for at least six months after the door handle on the driver's side broke for the umpteenth time and the salvage yards south of town ran out of replacements.) But the Firebird's most distinctive feature was its front end, which resembled the nose section of a fighter plane far more than the hood/grill/bumper of your average car. Indeed, like the old Model T, the Formula 400 *had no* front bumper to interfere with its sculpted beak and signature twin grilles.

When it came to power, the Formula 400 was a vehicle obviously conceived in madness. Even the most bare-bones version of the car came equipped with a 400-cubic-inch (hence the name "Formula 400"), 330-horsepower V8 aspirated by a four-barrel "Quadrajet" carburetor. Powered by this beast of a motor, the Formula 400 could go from 0 to 60 in six seconds flat and turn a quarter mile in fifteen seconds, reaching a top speed of 100 mph over that distance. But this is mere numerology. To truly understand what the numbers *400, 330, 0–60,* etc., portended, you had to find yourself a stretch of open road, strap on a seat belt (rarely used in those days), and proceed to put pedal to metal.

I'll never forget the first time my friends Jeff and Kent Green and I took the car cruising on Dodge City's Wyatt Earp Boulevard. "Dragging Earp," as this activity was affectionately called, was a long-standing tradition among the town's bored and restless youth. Generations of teens stretching all the way back to the days following World War II had taken part in the ritual. However, it was one thing to drag Earp in your father's F-150 or your mother's Buick wagon, as the Greens and I had been doing for a couple of years by then. It was quite another to take to the strip in a car like the Formula 400. Before, we'd felt mostly invisible, an insignificant speck on a drab and predictable scene, but now we *were* the scene. Girls who'd never given us the time of day flagged us down to ask for rides. Upperclassmen who'd never acknowledged our existence ambled over to inspect the car's six-speaker stereo and chrome-studded engine. Sitting behind the wheel of that glorious beast, we were utterly, completely transformed.

As that first night on Wyatt Earp wore on, an older, scrappier group of kids, some of whom had dropped out of school months or even years earlier, emerged on the boulevard. Sometime after eleven o'clock, I stopped at the light at Wyatt Earp and Fourteenth Street, and a greasy-haired kid in his late teens or early twenties pulled up beside me in a midnight-blue Plymouth Fury—shades of *Thunderbolt and Lightfoot*—and revved his engine.

"What the heck does *he* want?" I asked my friends over the blare of the stereo.

"To race, I think," Kent said.

"Really? Here?"

"I think so."

I revved my engine in response, the light turned from red to green, and the kid in the Fury burned off the line while I just sat there, shaking my head.

"What's the matter?" Jeff asked from the back seat. "Ain't you gonna race him?"

"Yeah, one of these days," I said.

"*One* of these days?"

"I need to . . . practice first."

"Practice?" Kent asked dismissively. "We're sitting here at this light, and you're talking about *practice?*"

I shrugged.

Half an hour later, we found ourselves on a dark country road (North Fourteenth, for those of you keeping score) with deep, grassy ditches on both sides and a mile of empty pavement stretched out before us. I switched off the Firebird's 8-track, which seconds before had been blasting Bob Seger's "Night Moves" at high volume, aimed the car down the centerline, and floored it. The Firebird took off like a rocket, engine roaring, tires belching black smoke. A quarter mile in, we hit the century mark—100 mph.

"Keep her going!" Kent yelled. "Bury that son of a bitch!"

What the hell, I thought, pressing the gas pedal all the way to the floor. 105, 110, 115. . . . By now, the car was shimmying and jumping all over the road, its suspension struggling to match the strength of that massive, chrome-studded engine. 118, 120. . . . I was terrified but exhilarated, too, and in a moment of youthful bravado, I reached down and switched on the stereo with its powerful equalizer and massive rear speakers. "*NIGHT MOVES!*" Bob Seger shrieked, and the sudden blast of that sound, together with the wind rushing into the Firebird on all sides, popped the rear window out of its rubber gasket and sent it cartwheeling through the air behind us.

"Holy shit!" Jeff yelled from the back seat, his hands reaching up instinctively to cover his head.

I glanced down at the speedometer, quivering somewhere south of 125 mph. The gas pedal still had another inch or two to go, but by now the shimmying had got to the point where I could barely keep the car out of the ditches.

"All right, all right," Kent yelled. "Back her off!"

I did as I was told, taking my foot completely off the gas and letting the car coast. "*Lord, I remember, Lord, I remember,*" Seger sang, his voice amplified almost beyond recognition.

I looked over at Kent and saw by the light of the moon that his hair was standing on end. So was Jeff's. So was mine.

"Well?" I asked, hands trembling on the steering wheel.

"Yeah," Kent answered in a tight voice. "Yeah, man. Hell, yeah."

We found the rear window amid the deep grasses of the roadside ditch, not a scratch on it. We popped the thing back into its rubber gasket, and just like that, the beast was whole again.

There were many such nights. Owning a car like the Formula 400 seemed to invite and inspire them. There was always another girl who wanted to go for a ride, another guy who wanted to test his jalopy against the Formula 400. After a while, it seemed like everyone in town knew the car. This included the cops, who appeared to resent the idea of a scrawny kid like me commanding such power and speed. Did I care what they, what anyone, thought? No, I did not. Instead, I burned through gasoline, tires, and traffic stops. One night, running from the police with the car's lights switched off, I drove through a wooden fence and onto the back nine of the country club golf course. Another time, my friend Tim Cook and I got the car stuck in a muddy field near Wright, Kansas, and had to ask the man whose daughters we'd sneaked out there to visit to pull us out with his 4010 John Deere.

"And just where in the hell am I supposed to hook *the chain?*" the man asked irritably, nodding at the car's beautiful, bumperless front end.

I laughed and shook my head sheepishly. I was damned if I knew.

Not once was the car used to haul babies or groceries or to take a sick pet to the veterinarian's office. Never did it pull a trailer or make a run to the airport to collect a visiting colleague. The Formula 400 was above such mundane matters. Its purpose was not transportation but transformation.

E. B. White hints at this theme of transformation in his 1936 essay "Farewell, My Lovely," where he writes, "The driver of the old Model T was a man enthroned." White was alluding to the Model T's height, which was said to be "seven-feet high with the top up." The low-slung Formula 400 was the exact opposite, and yet the effect it had on those lucky enough to slip behind its steering wheel was much the same.

One day during my freshman year at Dodge City Community College, I was working an evening shift at a truck stop south of town when a man in his early thirties spotted the Formula 400 in the parking lot and came inside the filling station.

"Who owns that green Firebird out there?" the man asked.

"I do," I answered, rising to my full height behind the counter.

The man paused, smiling in a knowing way. He was a heavily tanned guy in khakis and a polo shirt, with blond hair cropped close to his head. "I used to own that car," he said, "back when I was in high school."

"For real?" I said. "How do you know it's the same one?"

"Are you kidding?" he said, shaking his head ruefully. "You never really forget a car like that. I recognize every nick and dent in the body—or at least the ones I put there. What happened to the left rear quarter panel? Was it in a wreck or something?"

I nodded, and the man stood there another moment, his eyes glazed over as though lost in thought or memory. Then he took a business card out of his pocket and slid it across the counter to me. "If you ever want to sell her, give me a call."

"I don't see that happening," I said.

"I know you don't," he said. "I didn't, either. Just give me a call, okay?"

"Okay," I said.

I wish I could say I remembered to make that call when the time came for the Formula 400 and me to part ways, but life rarely works out that way. Instead, six months after leaving Dodge and moving to Lawrence, Kansas, I traded straight across for a boxy 1975 Volvo 242 without so much as saying a proper good-bye. What can I say? I was young and stupid and had reached the age where I figured I needed something a little more "sophisticated" to drive.

Not long ago, my son Jake and I were tooling around Jetmore, Kansas, a windblown hamlet eighteen miles north of my parents' ranch, when we came down a side street where a 1980 Pontiac Trans Am with mismatched tires and wheels sat beneath a shimmering cottonwood.

"Look at that!" Jake said breathlessly.

"I am," I said, pulling over.

"That thing is *sick!*"

"Yes, it is."

The car was white, like the Trans Am Jeff Bridges stole off that Montana car lot in *Thunderbolt and Lightfoot,* and it had the words OFFICIAL PACE CAR / *64th* ANNUAL *INDIANAPOLIS 500-MILE RACE* / *MAY 25, 1980* painted on its long, low doors.

I approached the car warily, knowing that its dark interior likely contained ghosts. Despite being a decade younger than my Formula 400, the Trans Am strongly echoed all of its most distinctive features, from the long, low doors to the beautiful, bumperless front beak. As we stood next to it in the grass, hands cupped against the windows, a teenager with spiked blond hair and earbuds came out of the house and approached us wordlessly. We, too, said nothing, but simply stepped back into the street and watched as the boy, who was maybe sixteen years old, opened the driver's side door and fell backwards into the bucket seat, the way you had to do when getting behind the wheel of that low-slung beast. A second later, he fired the car up and roared away, leaving us quite literally in the dust.

"Who the hell does he think *he* is?" my son asked.

"A man enthroned," I answered.

"What?"

"Nothing. Never mind."

The days were golden; the nights were dim and strange. I suppose it's time to say good-bye for real now. Farewell, my lovely.

—9—
Dog Heaven

Over the twenty-odd years we had been going there, my wife, Alyssa, and I had come to think of my family's 4,000-acre cattle ranch in southwest Kansas, where we spent a week every year between Christmas and New Year's (as well as a second week sometime around the end of July), as "dog heaven." By this we meant a couple of different things, some of them quite obvious and mundane (no fence or leash, fewer restrictions on the intake of dog chow), others almost mystical in their lack of internal coherence (Can dogs, who lack souls, in the theological sense of that word, even *go* to heaven, and if we somehow grant that they can, wouldn't they have to be *dead* in order to do so?). Mostly, though, we simply meant that the ranch was a place where a dog could go about the business of being a dog without being hovered over by a human being intent on taking away his freedom and replacing it with a dubious safety.

Living in a city as we did, Alyssa and I were well versed in the city way of owning and relating to a dog: the twice-daily walks at the end of a choke chain and leash; the picking up of poop in a plastic grocery bag recycled for the purpose; the hurried game of fetch with a tennis ball launched by a tennis racquet. It's not a bad life for a dog. The pounds and ASPCA offices of America are full of dogs that go to bed every night dreaming of just such a life. But still, if you were a dog, wouldn't you trade your cushy life in the city, if only for a week or two, for the life of a ranch dog, which includes, among other pursuits, gobbling kibble out of a hub cap, lapping water from a creek, chasing rabbits into deep, thorny cover, and keeping the coyotes at bay with your barking . . . all the while knowing, in the deepest part of your dog self, that it was *this* life and not your city dog life that you were really put on this earth to pursue?

This, at any rate, was the kind of anthropomorphism Alyssa and I indulged in every time we packed up our Jeep Cherokee with kids and dogs and headed off to spend time on the Lazy R Ranch, fourteen miles northeast of Dodge City. We loved the ranch. Our kids, Ria and Jake, loved the ranch. And of course our dogs—Blue, an elderly white Labrador retriever, and Trucker, a thirteen-inch beagle in his prime—loved the ranch, too. However, on a recent journey west, our collective love of the ranch was at once overshadowed and intensified by the fact that we all knew this would be Blue's last Christmas on the Lazy R.

We brought Blue home from the breeder's in Lexington, Kentucky, in February 2000, and in all the years since then, he'd been a willing, loyal, and mostly trouble-free companion, running off leash on the golf course near our home with Alyssa each morning, accompanying me on long walks most nights, submitting cheerfully to untold roughhousing on the part of all the kids in the neighborhood. In fact, the only real downside to life with Blue was the fact that he shed so much, leaving thick chunks of white hair plastered to every surface he came into contact with—furniture, carpeting, the legs of whatever pants (forget about black) one happened to be wearing at the time.

Loyalty and shedding aside, however, Blue's most pronounced trait had always been his deep and abiding dignity. Once, without meaning to, Alyssa happened to offend this towering dignity of Blue's, and although he loved her more than any creature, dog or human, on this earth, he never forgot the affront. What she did was dress him in human clothes—a pair of loose-fitting maternity jeans, if I remember correctly, and an old Brooklyn Dodgers hoodie—and then laugh. Of course, she regretted it instantly. For no sooner did Blue feel the full weight of her laughter than he turned, resolutely, away from her, his great white head facing the tile of the bathroom wall.

"Oh, Blue, I'm so sorry!" Alyssa said, hurrying to strip him of the offending garments. "I don't know what I was thinking! I promise I'll never do it again!"

But the damage was done. For weeks afterward, Blue wouldn't deign even to look at Alyssa. Or, if he did, it was only for a second, his sorrowful yellow eyes communicating the depth of his hurt.

The breeder in Lexington from whom we bought Blue had guaranteed the soundness of his hips and eyes (two hotspots of trouble for purebred Labs), and for the most part, he turned out to be a remarkably healthy dog. We didn't have a vet bill on him to speak of for the first six years of his life, and it was only after he turned nine or ten that he began to show signs of his age, and even then, the whiteness of his coat kept him from going gray in his muzzle the way most Labs do. But then the summer before he turned eleven, Alyssa noticed a mass growing on the back of his left thigh—a mass that eventually grew so large it had to be surgically removed. Tests on the tumor revealed that it had indeed been malignant; however, the vet who performed the surgery said there'd been no "stem" and that the "margins" surrounding the tumor were good, so there was at least some hope he'd make a full recovery.

"Can you believe what all this vet stuff costs?" I said to Alyssa. "Five hundred for the surgery, another two hundred for the tests. My God."

"I know," Alyssa agreed. "But at least he's still got a few good years left in him."

"Well, let's hope so," I said.

But it wasn't the money that bothered me. It was something far more fundamental than that. I knew that when the true end for Blue arrived, I wanted to preserve his dignity as much as possible and let nature run its course. No invasive surgery, chemo, or radiation, no getting guilted into seeking remedies that would only prolong his pain, not his life. "There's a point where you just have to say goodbye," I mused aloud.

Now, on the way west from Indianapolis to Dodge City, it began to seem more and more like the time had arrived to say good-bye. A couple of months earlier, two years after the initial cancer, Alyssa noticed a foul odor coming from Blue's mouth. I took a look (to the extent that he would let me), then loaded Blue into the back of the Jeep and took him to an animal hospital on the east side of Indianapolis. The vet there, Dr. Schnepf, did a full exam of Blue, and the news was not good. In addition to the growth in his mouth (almost certainly cancer), our thirteen-year-old Lab had arthritis in both knees and a blockage of some sort at the front of his lungs that made his breathing sound labored and heavy even when he wasn't exerting himself—a condition that had caused Alyssa to give Blue the affectionate nickname "Mr. Huff and Puff."

"Of course, we can run some tests if you want to," Dr. Schnepf said. "But given his age and everything else he has wrong with him, we'd be looking for a diagnosis, not a cure."

"So what do you suggest?"

"I can prescribe some antibiotics. That will help with the smell. Also some painkillers to make him more comfortable. Beyond that, it's a waiting game."

"How long?"

Here the vet scratched his beard thoughtfully. "Given what I'm seeing in his mouth, I don't think he has long, maybe another month or two. Three at the outside."

These were ominous words to hear, and in the days to come, Alyssa and I had several heart-wrenching talks. But no matter what direction these talks took, we always came back to the same point. If possible, we wanted to give Blue one more Christmas on the Lazy R. Hence the long drive west in a vehicle so full of the smell of death that we had to roll down the windows every fifteen miles in order to flush the cab with clean, cold highway air.

Unlike Blue, Trucker came to us already full-grown and set in his ways. In an earlier life, he'd been a show dog, living in a kennel in his breeder's garage and traveling to dog shows all over the country. He'd been successful enough at this life that the breeder, a woman Alyssa met through the AKC website, kept him on after his show career was over so that he could sire a new generation of beagle champions. However, several attempts to sire a litter (and some expensive lab work) later, it was determined that Trucker was "shooting blanks"—hence the breeder's offer to give the dog, free of charge, to a loving family.

He was a small dog, thirteen inches tall at the shoulder and about twenty pounds, and when we first drove out to meet him, he hid behind his breeder's legs, wanting nothing at all to do with us. When he was finally dragged out to meet Alyssa and the kids, his whole body shook as though he were freezing to death.

"He's a real sweetheart, just not used to people," the breeder observed. "His whole life has been about getting groomed, going to dog shows, and eating. But he'll warm up to you in a day or two."

I looked down at the shaking mass with its classic beagle looks—tricolor coat, floppy ears, tail that stood straight up from his butt.

"You mean he hasn't been living inside with you?" I asked, nodding at the door from the garage-kennel to the house proper.

"Well, we let him in sometimes," the breeder said. "He's a regular couch potato, in fact, and just loves to cuddle. But I wouldn't give any beagle the run of the house."

"You're saying he's not housebroken at all?" I asked. "How old is he?"

"I don't know off the top of my head. Five maybe? I can check his papers. And yes, he's housebroken. Just not completely, if you know what I mean."

I thought, *That's it. No way we're getting this dog.*

But then I looked down at the kennel floor, where Alyssa sat cross-legged holding Trucker in her arms. The kids could barely get a hand on him. "Isn't he adorable?" she said. "Look at the ticking on his paws. Oh my God, I love this dog."

And so that was that.

Life with Trucker—we didn't deign to change so perfect a name—was an adventure from the first. Within hours of bringing him home, he exploited an unseen weakness in our Cape Cod–style fence and went off "beagling"—no sign of him anywhere in the yard, no forwarding address. Alyssa freaked out and assembled a large search party to scour the neighborhood, but in the end, Trucker found his own way home, trotting up the back steps (where I'd left the door ajar) and into the living room with a supremely untroubled look on his face, as if to say, "Okay, I'm back. Where's the food?"

In time, the shyness we'd first observed in Trucker faded away. His favorite activity, after beagling and eating, was to lie in Alyssa's arms on the couch, eyes closed and feet pointing ceiling-ward, snoring loudly. We'd never had a small dog before—only big, athletic brutes like Blue and his predecessor, a chocolate Lab named Otis—and for this reason we were easily charmed. However, Trucker had his less-than-admirable qualities as well, not the least of them a habit of relieving himself on or in the personal belongings of anyone who happened to have raised his ire. Thus if Alyssa was a little slow to go on her morning jog on the golf course—an activity both dogs looked forward to with frantic anticipation—she might expect to find that Trucker had lifted his leg in her running shoes. Similarly, if I were fifteen or twenty minutes late with the kibble some morning or evening, I might wander into my office an hour or two later and find a collection of tiny, dried turds in my book bag.

"*What!?*" I'd howl. "Blue would never do such a thing!"

Angry, I'd chase the beagle down, rub his nose in the evidence of his crime, and kick his little butt into the backyard, where he'd shake himself off from ears to tail, find another hole in the fence to breach, and go beagling. The dog had no conscience at all. Guilt simply wasn't a part of his emotional repertoire.

We stopped for the night in Overland Park, Kansas, then continued westward, followed, as we often were when we went to the ranch, by Alyssa's mother, Andra, and her poodle-terrier mix, Lucky. It was December 23, Alyssa's birthday, and we celebrated with burgers and ice cream in Hutchinson. By the time we arrived at the Lazy R, it was already dark. We'd come 840 miles in two days, accompanied the whole way by the terrible stench of Blue's illness, but the reward for having made the drive would be eight uninterrupted days on the ranch. As an added bonus, the weather forecast for the first half of our stay was glorious—blue skies, very little wind, temperatures in the mid-forties. Perfect weather for a winter stay on the ranch.

The next morning, while I fed horses and broke ice out of the water tank, Alyssa went on her usual morning run with dogs in tow. This was always a sizable entourage, for in addition to our two dogs and Lucky, several of the dogs in residence on the Lazy R usually insisted on going, too. These included, at different times, Cassie, a young Siberian Husky, very much the leader of the pack; Snookers, an older, sausage-shaped beagle; Sierra, an orange-coated Chow mix; Cracker, a big yellow Lab who was even older than Blue; and Sadie, a skittish greyhound mix. The ranch dogs were largely outdoor dogs, sleeping in the yard or under the porch during the summer and in three heated, igloo-shaped doghouses during the winter. Some of these dogs had been adopted from a local shelter. Others, like Cassie, were what my father liked to call "volunteers," having gotten lost or, more likely, dumped in the country before showing up on the ranch. Whatever their origin, they all seemed to adapt readily to ranch life, leading Alyssa and me to wonder how well Blue and Trucker would adapt, if given the chance. The longer we stayed on the ranch, the more we began to treat our city dogs the way we treated the ranch dogs—leaving them outside all day, not bothering to put a leash on them during their long runs with Alyssa, trusting them to find their way home whenever they got separated from the pack. These were small adjustments—both dogs slept inside with us, rather than on the porch, and whenever we went into town, we always locked them up in their crates in the ranch house—but they felt big to us.

It was for one last taste of ranch life that we'd hauled Blue across the states of Indiana, Illinois, Missouri, and Kansas. And on that first morning on the Lazy R, running with Alyssa and his ranch dog buddies, he seemed almost like his old self. He gave it a shot, anyhow, pushing himself to keep up with the pack for at least the first part of the run before Alyssa had to cut it short in order to bring him back. However, that single morning run turned out to be Blue's last hurrah, and he paid for it dearly. By late afternoon he was so gimped up and sore I had to double his pain medication, and the following morning, when Alyssa got ready for her run, Blue balked at going, refusing to move from his bed by the fire.

"Are you sure, Blue?" Alyssa prodded him. "It's not that cold. You had so much fun yesterday!"

But Blue just looked away, hiding his honey-colored eyes.

In days to come, he did little more than eat and sleep. At other times he'd wander aimlessly around the ranch house, as though lost or looking for something. Or he'd circle and circle, as though preparing to lie down, but then he'd pause, seeming to forget, and would have to begin the whole process over again.

"I don't know," I said to Alyssa. "I think we may be getting near the end."

"What are you saying?" she asked suspiciously.

"Do you really want to haul a dying dog all the way back to Indianapolis, after all the trouble we took getting him this far?"

"What other choice do we have?"

I paused before going any further. "We could have him put down here. Bury him on the ranch, at Owl Rock, or one of his other favorite places."

"I'm not ready for that," Alyssa said.

"I'm not either, exactly. But it's something we need to think about. The forecast says it's going to snow in a day or two. If the ground freezes. . . ."

"I know all that," Alyssa said. "But I want to wait all the same."

Even with Blue out of commission, Alyssa still had plenty of company on her morning runs. Trucker and Lucky continued to go until

Andra went back to Kansas City the day after Christmas, and among the ranch dogs, Cassie and Snookers could always be counted on, although they were just as likely to break off from the pack mid-run to pursue a jack rabbit or run a coyote off the place. These jaunts of theirs were a pleasure to see and to hear—Cassie bounding through the tall grass to close the gap between herself and a fleeing deer, and Snookers "sounding the alarm" in his squeaky beagle voice. More pleasurable still was seeing Trucker or Lucky join in the fun. Though never one to initiate the chase, once Trucker heard Snookers's baying, the beagle in him could not resist adding his voice—and his nose and legs—to the chase. And once he'd taken off with the other dogs, you could pretty much forget about calling him back. For despite his diminutive size and show-dog breeding, at the end of the day, he was still a beagle—all nose. Like Snookers and the other ranch dogs, he'd have to find his own way back after the hunt was over. This might mean his showing up at the corrals or ranch house before Alyssa even returned from her run, or it might mean that two or even three hours passed before he trotted down from some far-off plateau, fur covered in stickers or mud, tongue hanging almost to the ground.

"Trucker boy!" Alyssa or one of the kids would yell in greeting. "Where have you been? Did you have fun? We were about to give you up for dead!"

Then, on December 29, a little over halfway through our stay on the Lazy R, Alyssa and Ria went on a long run on the highest part of the ranch's back pasture. It was another gorgeous day, and as usual they saw an abundance of wildlife—jack rabbits, coyotes, a herd of twenty or so deer. It was the deer, Alyssa said later, that caused Snookers to sound the alarm, and soon both he and Trucker had taken off after them in hot pursuit.

"There they go," Alyssa remarked, shaking her head. She and Ria called after the dogs a few times, but as usual this proved to be a pointless task, and so after a few minutes, they left the two beagles to their business and continued on without them.

I was on a ride in another pasture when my phone buzzed with a text message from Ria. "Look for Trucker while you're riding."

"Will do," I texted back, thinking little of it.

It was 1:30 or 2:00 p.m., and there was plenty of time for beagles to return from beagling. After I finished that first solo ride of the day, Ria and Jake and I saddled up and went out again. The weather was spectacular—blue skies, no wind, forty or forty-five degrees. We had a wonderful time, perhaps our best ride of the entire trip, playing a game of horseback tag in one of the pastures on the south side of the ranch, and we were all smiles and laughs as we came down through the bluffs just across the road from the ranch house. Only then, with the tack barn in sight, did I fish my phone from my pocket and call Alyssa.

"Trucker turn up?"

"No," Alyssa said. "It's been four hours. He's never been gone this long before."

"What about Snookers? Has he come home?"

"Yes, about an hour ago," Alyssa said. "He was covered in mud from head to tail. God only knows what they got into."

"Where exactly did you see them last?"

"In the high part of the back pasture. They crossed under the fence, headed north. I was just up there again, looking for him. He's gone from there now."

"All right," I said. "I'll go have a look, too. Call me if he turns up."

We unsaddled the horses and got them fed and watered, then Ria and Jake and I jumped into the Cherokee, crossed the dam over Sawlog Creek, and drove into the back pasture to have a look. It was that time of day when the sky is dark blue and shadows fall long across the land. A half-mile into the pasture, the terrain became more rugged, and I got the Jeep high-centered trying to cross a tumbleweed-choked ravine. While I waited for Chris, the main hired man on the ranch, to come and pull me out, I sent Ria and Jake to scour ravines in the adjoining pasture where the dogs had last been seen. Soon both of them were mere specks on the horizon, their voices swallowed whole by the surrounding landscape.

After Chris towed me out of the ravine, we picked up Ria and Jake and covered several square miles north and west of the ranch. Noticing a familiar biplane flying overhead, Chris called a friend who relayed a message about Trucker to the pilot. A few minutes later, a search from the air began, with the pilot passing low over the land several times before tipping his wings apologetically and continuing on his way. In an hour of looking, we saw no sign at all of Trucker, and as dusk began to fall, we had to call the search off.

We were expected in town for dinner with my parents, and since there was nothing more we could do to help Trucker that day, we kept the date. The conversation that night was heavy on lost dogs past and present.

"Cassie and Snookers were missing for more than a week this past fall," my father remarked. "Then a neighbor called and said he'd seen them at an abandoned ranch. We pulled up in the yard of the place, and there they were. Cassie was glad to see us, but Snookers acted like he didn't care if he went home or not."

"Remember Kashmir?" I asked, invoking the memory of a legendary family dog of twenty-five years earlier. "What's the longest he was gone?"

"Oh, that dog was always running off," my mother said. "He'd be gone for weeks at a time, sometimes months. Then he'd show up again, half-dead from his travels, little more than skin and bones. Once he came back with a different collar and tag on. Someone had picked him up, and he was their dog for a while, but he got away and came back to live with us."

I stole glances across the table at Alyssa as these stories were told. I could tell they weren't making her feel any better about Trucker.

"Anyway, it's supposed to be a really mild night," my father said. "If he isn't back in the morning, we'll drive out and look in a couple of places I know about. I already called the neighbors, and they'll let us know if he turns up."

We drove back to the ranch in silence. Once there, we sat up before a fire in the living room, Alyssa getting up to look out the window every few minutes. Blue came up and demanded to be petted. The smell from his mouth was worse than ever. It was strange to sit there in the warm glow of the fireplace, knowing that Trucker was somewhere out there on the dark prairie.

"Where do you suppose he is?" Alyssa asked.

"I don't know. Hunkered down somewhere would be my guess."

"Tell me the truth. Do you think a coyote got him? I saw one in the field where he disappeared right before he and Snooks took off."

"No," I said. "Coyotes are afraid of dogs. My guess is he'll be back by morning, demanding his breakfast."

The whole night through, Alyssa kept hearing dogs barking at the coyotes across the road from the ranch house. Each time it happened, she got out of bed and went outside to see if the barking dog was Trucker, only to find Cassie or Sadie or Sierra looking up at her with quizzical expressions, as if to ask, *What are you doing out here in the middle of the night? It's not time to run yet, is it?*

The next day dawned clear and cold. Shortly after breakfast, my father and Jake and I set out in one of the ranch Jeeps to see if Trucker had sought refuge at the old Holliday place, an abandoned ranchstead located a couple of miles north of the ranch. Even getting to this old homestead, which was tucked into a valley miles from any road, proved to be a challenge. Opening a gate at the northeast corner of the ranch, we passed into an empty pasture and continued along a bumpy ranch road—little more than a couple of tire ruts in the grass—until we came to a deep ravine and, crossing that, to a gateless, four-wire fence.

"The Holliday place is in the next valley to the north," my father said. "You'll see the house and the windmill when you top the hill above the place. I'll wait here until you get back." At nearly eighty years old, having endured double knee and hip replacement, he was not up to the kind of walking we were about to do.

"Okay," I said. "We'll be quick."

A mile into our hike, we topped a high plateau and there it lay in the valley below us—a small, square house dating from the 1880s set alongside a winding creek with tall cottonwoods and smaller cedar trees growing on either side. Looking down on the little house in its hidden valley, I almost expected to see a column of smoke rising from its derelict chimney. Wasn't that always the way in those Hollywood Westerns I used to watch as a kid? Didn't the searchers always arrive at just such a house, in just such a valley, in just such a moment as this, starving, lost, with a bad storm blowing in? Didn't the next scene invariably show the searchers warming themselves before a crackling fire?

Yes, but that's not the way it was for Jake and me. After walking another half mile and crossing the frozen creek, we spent only a few minutes inspecting the house with its half-boarded windows and fallen-in ceiling and kitchen furniture from another era (pie safe, Hoosier cabinet, kerosene stove) before we continued our search amid the trees farther up the frozen creek, our voices echoing amid the cottonwoods and cedars, "Truck-er, oh Truck-er, here Truckerboy!"

Deeper in those trees, we came upon a patch of flattened grass with a picked-clean deer carcass at its center.

"What is this place?" Jake asked.

"Coyote's den," I answered, pointing to the places amid the dead cottonwood leaves where the coyotes had shed their steely fur.

"Did they kill this deer? Did they *eat* it?" Jake asked, reaching out with his booted foot to move the deer's antlers back and forth.

"Ate, yes," I said. "Killed? Well, maybe. Coyotes are scavengers. They're like buzzards that way. For them to kill an animal this big would take four or five of them working together in a pack. I just don't see that."

We stood there another moment, neither of us willing to mention the grisly math we were doing in our brains. If a grown deer weighing two or three hundred pounds could be brought down and killed—

or even dragged here and eaten—then what about a twenty-pound beagle?

"Come on," I said finally. "Let's head back. Grandpa's waiting for us."

In what remained of that morning, we searched one far-flung part of the ranch after another. Owl Rock. The Adams pasture. The sprinklers north of Antelope Road. The bull pasture. Chester's. All to no avail. We looked again in the afternoon, and yet again in the dusk of early evening. Again to no avail. That night, a norther blew in. Temperatures plummeted, and it began to snow.

"He was so innocent," Jake said, choking back tears. "He didn't deserve any of this."

Ria and I looked at each other, both of us noting his use of past tense.

"I know he was," Alyssa answered. "He was a good dog, and we should've taken better care of him."

"It's nobody's fault," I said. "He was doing something he loved, and he got turned around and lost, that's all."

We stayed together a few minutes longer, then Alyssa went downstairs to try to get some sleep, while I sat up before a fire, watching through the living-room window as the snow continued to fall out of the night sky. I'd found my way to that house in the valley where the searchers in sentimental Westerns always find solace and rest, but alas, poor Trucker hadn't. He'd taken a wrong turn somewhere, headed off in the wrong direction, and whatever hope remained that he'd somehow smell his way back to the ranch was being buried now under the accumulating snow.

On the morning of New Year's Eve, we got up later than usual and moped around the ranch house as though uncertain what to do with ourselves. I dragged out Blue's bowl and filled it with kibble, but for the first time in his life he couldn't finish his breakfast. He tried, but his knees kept buckling, forcing his head up and his butt to the floor. It was a terrible sight to behold. At last he gave up altogether and just stood there, huffing and puffing in that way he had that was familiar now without being at all natural.

"Poor Blue," I heard myself say. It was what all of us had begun to say. *Poor Blue, poor Blue, poor Blue.*

Of all of us, Alyssa was the hardest hit by Trucker's disappearance. She talked openly of skipping our traditional New Year's Eve celebration with my family in town, saying she'd prefer to stay on the ranch by herself. I couldn't believe what I was hearing.

"Don't you think that's just a little bit selfish of you?" I asked. "It's still New Year's Eve. What about me and the kids? What about my parents?"

"I'm sorry, but I just don't feel like celebrating. I'm not like the rest of you. I can't pretend I'm happy when I'm not."

"Who's asking you to pretend? Just come along with the rest of us, and when someone asks how you're feeling, tell them the truth. They'll understand."

"It's not that simple."

"Sure it is," I said. "Do you think we're the first people to lose a dog? We're not. Not by a long shot."

Later, as I was pulling on my boots to feed and water the horses, Alyssa appeared at the back door in boots and running clothes.

"I'm heading to the back pasture to look for Trucker," she said. "You can come with me if you want to, but if you don't, that's fine, too. I'll go alone."

"You really think you're going to find him?" I asked. "There's at least four inches of snow out there. On top of that, the wind is picking up."

"I have to do *something*," she said. "Even if I just find his collar, or the place where it happened, that will be better than this."

"Wait until I've broken ice and fed the horses."

"No, *you* wait," she said. "I'm out of here."

Angry, I rifled through a pack of snow gear and came up with a pair of gaiters dating from our cross-country skiing days. "At least put these on and wear a heavy coat," I said, before heading out the door.

I found the horses waiting for me at the front of the corral, their shoulders and backs wet from the snow. Using a hammer and a trenching spade, I broke the ice out of their water trough, then hauled a sack of grain from the tack barn and began feeding them, making sure their feed buckets were spread far apart so that the dominant horses wouldn't keep the weaker ones from eating. As I was feeding, a big gust of wind came through the corrals from the north, scooping snow from the ground and throwing it high into the air, so that visibility dropped to a hundred yards and then to fifty. I thought of Alyssa and her morbid errand at the high end of the back pasture. *What if the wind picks up even more, and she gets turned around and lost like Trucker? How will I ever explain the fact that I let her go?*

Worried now, I took my cell phone from my pocket and dialed Alyssa's number. The phone rang a half dozen times before going to voice mail. I knew my wife. She'd never checked a voice mail in her life, so I didn't even bother leaving one. Instead, I climbed into the ranch Jeep and gunned it through the snow from the corrals back to the ranch house, redialing Alyssa's number every few moments. The last time I dialed it, I was on my way into the kitchen from the back steps, and before her phone even stopped ringing, I had it in my hands and switched it to mute.

"Goddamn it, Alyssa," I said aloud.

The snow in the back pasture was so deep I had to keep the Jeep in the low range of four-wheel drive just to plow my way through it. There was less snow at the top of the pasture, but the visibility up there was far worse—fifty or sixty yards at most. Alyssa and whatever dogs she'd taken with her were nowhere in sight. I drove along the northern fence line of the pasture, honking the Jeep's horn the entire way, but turned up nothing—no sign of Alyssa or the dogs, no answer to my honking.

Was it possible she had turned back without my seeing her? I doubted that.

I backtracked to the east fence line and got out of the Jeep to look for tracks. After a few minutes, I found them, already half filled with blowing snow. The tracks headed north along the fence line, crossing the northern boundary of the ranch near the place my father and I had crossed on our way to the Holliday place. I opened the corner gate and continued a mile and a half until the high, flat part of the pasture gave out to deep ravines. There I turned the Jeep off and scanned what I could see of the horizon with a pair of binoculars. Aside from the rippling of the land and a couple of deep, tree-lined ravines, there was nothing to see but whiteness and snow and more whiteness and snow. A famous passage from Melville came to me unbidden: "by its indefiniteness it shadows forth the heartless voids and immensities of the universe, and thus stabs us from behind with the thought of annihilation."

A moment later, I picked up a flash of movement at the edge of the binoculars. It was Cassie, her black Siberian coat standing out strongly against the white. Then Snookers, nose down and ears flopping. And finally, coming up out of a low spot behind both dogs, Alyssa's brown parka. I lowered the binoculars and sat there a moment, gathering myself. I could feel the anger and fear leaving my body like air from a balloon, the space they'd occupied replaced by gratitude. Climbing down from the Jeep, I walked into the high, windblown pasture to where my slack-faced, grieving wife was looking for the bodily remains of a dog that by then had been missing for more than forty-eight hours.

"He's gone," I said. "You'll never find him in all this."

"That's easy for you to say. You didn't lose him."

"Neither did you. He ran off, that's all."

"No, that's not right."

"Yes, it is."

She tried to walk away, but I grabbed both of her shoulders and held her. "Do you know what it's going to look like out here if that wind really gets going? It'll be a total whiteout. We won't be able to see our hands in front of our faces."

"I doubt that," she said.

"Well, you shouldn't. There are two kids back at that ranch house who need their mother, and I need her, too."

I tried to pull her into a hug. She resisted it at first, then relaxed bodily in my arms. "I wasn't lost," she said into my ear. "I told you where I was going, and I had the dogs with me."

"I know all that," I said. "I was worried about you, that's all. I'm still worried."

We stood there with the snow swirling around us until we began to grow cold, and then we coaxed Cassie and Snookers into the Jeep and headed back to the ranch.

On New Year's Day, we packed the Cherokee's roof rack, loaded Blue into the back, and left the ranch on icy roads, headed for Kansas City. The night before, at a subdued New Year's Eve celebration in town, my parents had promised to keep looking for Trucker.

"Adam is coming back from Topeka for a week," my mother said, referring to my brother Dave's son. "He and Chris will keep an eye out for him, and we'll run an ad in the *Globe,* too."

Alyssa and I looked at each other, both of us thinking the same thing. *They're crazy. Don't they know that our sweet beagle is in the belly of a coyote now? Haven't they come to terms with that?*

Everyone we saw in Kansas City had kind things to say about Trucker and Blue. Trucker had died doing something he loved doing, and Blue had lived a long and good life. It was all true—as far as it went.

On the morning of January 3, we packed up the Jeep one last time and set out on the final five-hundred-mile leg of our journey. Alyssa spent the first hour of the trip fiddling with her phone, and when I asked her what she was doing, she admitted that she was visiting the web sites of various dog breeders.

"I know they say it's better to wait a while when you've lost a dog, but I can't. The thought of Blue being gone, and Trucker, too. . . . I'm sorry, but I don't know if I can handle that."

"You don't have to explain yourself," I said. "I feel the same way."

Here Alyssa paused a moment. "I feel like I didn't respect the ranch," she said. "I didn't recognize the power and danger of it. I acted like it was some kind of city park, but that's not what it is at all, and I should've known better. Believe me, I won't make the same mistake again."

Again we were on the same page. I'd been thinking exactly the same thing.

We arrived home in Indianapolis on a Thursday night. On Friday, I called the animal hospital to see about getting Blue put down. They could see him that afternoon or before noon on Saturday, but they wouldn't be open on Sunday. On Monday, Ria and Jake started a new semester at school. By now, Blue was barely touching his food, and his breathing had grown even more labored. All of the spark had gone out of his eyes, and he no longer wagged his tail when Alyssa called his name.

I called the family together in the kitchen. "It's time to say good-bye to Blue," I said. There were tears, of course, but not as many as with Trucker, for we'd all seen this moment coming for a long time. The good-byes said, I loaded Blue into the back of the Jeep for the final time, and as tears streamed down the faces of those I loved most in the world, I reversed out of the driveway and headed off, alone, to the animal hospital.

There, Blue and I were led into a room on the south side of the building with a big frosted window with sun beaming through it. After a short wait, Dr. Schnepf walked in. "I can tell he's worse by the smell alone," he said. He performed an abbreviated version of the exam he'd done on Blue five weeks earlier, shaking his head and frowning the whole time. "You were right to bring him in," he said. "It's time."

He asked if I wanted to be in the room while Blue was put down, and I told him I did. Together we lifted Blue onto the metal exam table, and I stood over him kneading the muscles in his shoulders as

Dr. Schnepf shaved the fur from his right front leg. With the hair gone, he found a vein and inserted an IV line and drew some of Blue's blood into the long tube where the drugs would be injected.

"Ready?"

I nodded, still kneading Blue's shoulders, great clumps of his white hair covering my hands and the sleeves of my shirt the way it always did when I petted him. Dr. Schnepf injected a tranquilizer into the tube first, then followed that with a second drug, the one that would stop Blue's heart and give him the peace he deserved.

"Okay, let's ease him back."

Supporting his massive white head in the crook of my arm, I eased Blue down until he was on his side on the metal table, the sun streaming through the frosted windows to light up his white coat. He hadn't let out so much as a sigh during the whole procedure.

I had just stepped back from the table to take a final picture of Blue with my phone when it buzzed in my hand and I looked blankly at the name on the screen. It was my nephew Adam.

"Stay with him as long as you like," Dr. Schnepf said, gathering his things to go.

"Thank you," I said. "I appreciate everything you've done."

The vet nodded gravely and left the room. I debated a second whether to answer the call, but something told me I should.

"Hello? Rob?"

"Yes?" I said. "What is it?"

"Dude, you're not going to believe this, but we just found Trucker."

"Found Trucker?" I repeated. "What do you mean you found him?"

"Chris and I spotted him on the road to town. We've got him right here in the pickup. The little sumbitch bit me, too."

"What?" I said, still not comprehending. "You're saying he's alive?"

"Hell, yes, he's alive," Adam laughed. "Didn't I just say he bit me? His paws look terrible and he's a little skinny, but otherwise there's not a mark on him."

I stood there in the sun-splashed room, struggling to take in this news, as Adam explained how earlier that day Chris and my father had spotted Trucker running on a sand road a couple of miles southwest of the ranch, but had not been able to catch him. An hour later, Chris and Adam returned to the spot, which was in a bend in the road near some abandoned farm buildings, and this time, when they spotted Trucker running along the road, Adam jumped from the moving pickup and chased him into an open field and tackled him.

"That's when he bit me," Adam said. "You didn't tell me the little sumbitch was dangerous."

"How do you suppose he stayed alive all this time?" I asked. "It's been almost a week."

"Who knows?" Adam responded. "Ask Grandma Pat, and she'll tell you it's because she lit a candle at the seven o'clock Mass this morning."

"Don't call or text Alyssa," I said. "I want to be the one to tell her."

"All right," Adam said. "I'm just glad he turned up."

"So am I," I said.

After the call ended, I stood there a long time, marveling at the strangeness of it all, how Blue had breathed his last breath at almost the exact moment when news of Trucker's improbable survival reached me. Later, when I told her about it, Ria was similarly struck by this sequence of events. Although neither of us was the sort to believe in such things, it was almost as though Blue, his great nobility intact to the end, had given his life so that the dog that had been brought into the family to replace him could live. It was a crazy thought, but inescapable, too.

I had a phone call to make. But first I switched on my phone and snapped a photo of Blue where he lay on the sunlit table. I felt slightly morbid doing it, but I wanted something more than the smell of death and Trucker's reappearance to remember him by.

"Good-bye, old friend," I said. "If there's a heaven for dogs, I'm sure you're there."

–10–
A Horse in the Country

Almost from the day we moved to Indianapolis in the summer of 1998, my wife, Alyssa, and I had been talking about how nice it would be to have a horse in the country. Horses had been a big part of my life ever since I began riding as a teenager in western Kansas, but my later life as a graduate student and then as an assistant professor in a large urban university never provided the mix of time, money, and proximity to the country that was necessary for keeping a horse. In a quarter century of riding, I'd acquired all manner of tack, including three or four saddles and a closet full of bridles and bits, but I'd never once owned or kept a horse, and for the most part, this state of affairs had suited me just fine. I could go months without riding or even thinking about horses. Then when the opportunity to visit my family's ranch in western Kansas arose, as it did every Christmas and for a week or two every summer, I'd morph into a horse-obsessed maniac who rode five or six hours a day. Witnessing this transformation, Alyssa would wonder aloud why we couldn't live a more "normal" life without all this "switching back and forth" between our country and city identities.

"Why not break down and get a horse or two of our own?" she'd ask.

"Two reasons," I'd answer. "Time and money. I don't have the time, and we don't have the money."

Then my brother Joe, who lived in suburban Kansas City and had never expressed much interest in riding, suddenly bought a Palomino gelding along with a pickup and trailer and 120 acres of grass where he could ride and play the role of weekend rancher. The horse turned out to be a dud, but this did nothing to dampen Joe's growing enthusiasm for all things equine. He bought a string of better horses, upgraded the pickup and trailer, and broke ground on a new stable and indoor riding arena.

I watched these developments from afar with a mixture of envy and amusement. All those years I'd spent mastering the role of horseless cowboy, Joe had been slaving away atop a glass tower in downtown Kansas City, and the result, now that we were both past forty, was that while I was still ahead of Joe as a rider, he'd jumped out far in front of me in what he liked to call, employing a phrase no doubt acquired at Tractor Supply, "animal husbandry." And given all the riding he was doing, it was only a matter of time before he passed me in that area, too.

Obviously, something had to be done.

A couple of years before this, during a yearlong hiatus from teaching, I'd done some riding at a full-service barn in the countryside thirty minutes from my house on the east side of Indianapolis. Once a week I'd drive out to the stable, ride for half an hour, and then make the half-hour return trip. Add it all up, and I was spending a lot more time behind the wheel of my Jeep than I was in the saddle, and I knew that once I returned to my normal teaching schedule I'd no longer have that kind of time to throw around. If I wanted to keep riding, I was either going to have to move to the country (an option that was not exactly in the cards) or find another stable closer to home. "Under ten miles—and closer to five." That's what I kept coming back to every time I considered the problem.

An Internet search turned up two possibilities. The first was a full-service barn with a price tag of $350 a month. Here the barn owner supplied the hay and took care of all the feeding and watering and cleaning of stalls. All the horse owner did was "show up and ride." The second place, a so-called "rider's co-op," was just $150 a month. Here horse owners supplied their own hay and shouldered their share of the feeding, watering, and stall-cleaning responsibilities.

One day, after talking horses with Joe for the better part of an hour,

I drove out to take a look at the co-op, which was located on a country lane seven miles from my house. I drove past the place twice before I realized there was no sign to speak of, just a house number stenciled on a black mailbox. On the right side of the ten-acre property, perhaps a hundred yards from the road, stood a ranch-style house with a trailered ski boat parked in the driveway. On the left, at a similar distance from the road, was a handsome, 60' × 120' metal barn. Parking just inside the gravel drive, I got out and walked in that direction. At the front of the barn, a doorway big enough to drive a truck through stood open. I stepped inside and waited a second for my eyes to adjust to the dim light. From what I could see, the barn contained a couple of tack rooms and cross tie areas along with stalls for a dozen or so horses. Stretching from door to door in the middle of the building was a plowed arena big enough to lope a horse in an oblong circle. Wafting about the air was the familiar smell of a horse barn in wet-weather country—a mixture of manure, dirt, moldy wood, and hay. Although most people, particularly those with allergies, would have found this smell off-putting, to me it was deeply satisfying. A little too wet to be the smell of home, perhaps, but close. Damn close.

Behind the barn, the property opened up into a series of small pastures with a central alley connecting them. In one pasture, a white Shetland pony nursed her colt, while in the far back pasture, a half dozen saddle horses, a mixture of Arabians and Standardbreds, stood watching me over the top rail of the fence, tails swishing noisily at flies. Taking in this scene, I felt more in touch with the world of my childhood than I had anywhere but in southwest Kansas. It was as though a smaller version of that world—a kind of branch office—had opened its doors before me.

"You know, this just might work," I heard myself say.

Meanwhile, back in Kansas, the stars were aligning themselves in such a way as to suggest that God had decided I needed a horse in Indianapolis. Dave McCollum, the head of the animal science program at

Dodge City Community College, called Joe to say that he had a sea-
soned show horse he needed to get out of his barn, and Joe promptly
reported the conversation to me. "Sounds like a good horse. Twelve
years old, lots of training. Dave says he moves really well for a big
horse. And the price is right, too."

"How much?"

"From what McCollum says, we can probably get him bought for
under a thousand. Maybe even seven-fifty."

"What's the catch?"

"There isn't one. Apparently the owner left the country. No forwarding address—just a cell phone number and a barn bill that's getting bigger by the day. Think you're interested?"

"Maybe."

"Have you got a place to keep him?"

"I think so."

"What about a trailer?"

"I'd need to buy one."

"How about this," Joe said, pausing to consider the matter. "You
buy the trailer, and I'll buy the horse. If everything works out and you
like him, you can buy him from me for whatever I paid. If not, I'll
bring him back to my barn, or we can leave him at the ranch."

Wow, I thought. Had Joe become so evangelical about animal husbandry that he was willing to float me the price of the horse just so
he could chalk up another convert? "All right," I said. "Let's get him
bought."

I already had my eye on a trailer. It was an old, two-horse bumper-
pull that had sat in a driveway a few blocks from my house for as long
as I could remember. After getting off the phone with Joe, I walked
down the street to take a closer look. The trailer was a peculiar looking contraption—all black with a ramp that came down in the back,
English style. I searched without luck for a brand name or serial number, then knocked at the front door of the house where the trailer was
parked and talked briefly to an older woman who told me that it might
be for sale.

"My husband bought that thing years ago to move furniture," she said. "It's never had a horse in it that I've ever seen. But go ahead and leave your phone number, and I'll have him call you."

When I told Alyssa about the trailer, she was immediately skeptical. "That old black thing down the street? You're going to buy *that*? How do you know it works?"

"It's a trailer," I said. "If the floor is sound and the wheels move, it works."

A day or two after this, I hooked the trailer to my Jeep Cherokee and set out for a test drive. The doors above the ramp came loose and flapped loudly in the wind, and only a few of the running lights worked, but the trailer tracked straight enough, and the Jeep had no trouble pulling it.

"What will you take for it?" I asked the owner, a man of retirement age who apparently had lived in the neighborhood as long as I had without our ever having crossed paths.

"Pretty hard to buy a horse trailer for less than fifteen hundred," he began.

"That's true," I said. "But this one is old, and it needs work on the doors and lights. I could offer you nine hundred, tops."

"Twelve and we'll call it a deal."

"Eleven."

"Oh, all right," the man said, smiling. "Since you want it so bad."

When I parked the trailer in front of my house, a neighbor from across the street came out into her yard with a look of amazement in her eyes.

"What's this? Are you getting a horse?"

"It would appear so, yes."

"Really? Where are you gonna keep it?"

"In the country."

"The trailer, too, I hope?" she asked, laughing nervously.

"That's the plan," I said, although it was fast occurring to me that I didn't really have a plan, but was only feeling my way toward one. I was like a newlywed man who'd just been told that he was about to become a father. There was that same mix of exhilaration and dread.

It's really happening, I thought. *Before it was just an idea, but now there's actual money involved.*

Things moved quickly after that. Joe bought the horse, which we decided to call "Red," and I dropped $350 on lights and new door latches for the black trailer. I called the woman listed as owner of the stable I'd visited and left my cell number for her to call me back. A couple of minutes passed, and then a text message lit up the tiny screen on my phone.

> Got yr message. The barn's a coop.
> R u ok with that? If yes, give me
> yr email and Ill send barn rules.

This was in the days before text messages became so widespread, and I remember being a little startled and put off. Still, I answered with my e-mail address, and not long after that the barn rules— fourteen pages, single-spaced!—arrived in my inbox.

The next day I dropped a check for the first month's rent (plus another month's security deposit) in the mailbox at the barn and parked the black trailer next to the manure wagon. Seeing that wagon with the ramp running up to it gave me some pause, I will admit—another of those flashes of dread that first-time fathers are prone to (*You mean to tell me I'm gonna have to change diapers?*)—but for the most part I felt smugly satisfied by the whole arrangement. Not only had I found a barn close to home, but at $150 a month, the place was dirt cheap.

And so, one Friday in June, I pulled the black trailer five hundred miles across Indiana, Illinois, and Missouri, arriving in Kansas City just as the evening rush hour was drawing to a close. Joe met me at a stable on the Missouri side where he'd been keeping Red ever since our father delivered him from Dodge City. Pulling into the long driveway of the stable, I immediately spotted Red standing in the round pen, a tall, long, reddish-colored horse (hence the name) with a single white blaze on his face and four stocking feet. *Wow, big horse*, I remember thinking.

"So this is the mystery trailer," Joe said as I stepped out of the Jeep to shake his hand. "Let's have a look."

We walked in a semi-circle around the trailer, starting at the front, where a side door allowed access to a storage compartment that ran the width of the trailer. "What are you gonna put in there?" Joe asked.

"I don't know. Hay, probably."

Hearing this, Joe immediately started for the barn behind us. "Let's grab a few bales and see how they fit."

We dragged a couple of fifty-pound bales of alfalfa from the barn and loaded them into the compartment.

"Nice," Joe said.

The inspection continued, my brother commenting on the trailer's height and the state of its tires and wheels before he stopped short at the sight of the ramp.

"I don't like the looks of that."

"What? Why not?"

"The wood looks half rotten. See how they've reinforced it with these angle irons?"

I kicked one of the irons with the heel of my boot. "Oh, it'll be fine."

"How do you know? Have you tested it?"

"I've walked up and down it a few times."

"Yeah, and you weigh, what, two hundred pounds? Red weighs six times that."

"Fine," I said, irritated by these questions. "Let's get to testing."

While Joe stood watching, I dropped the ramp down with a thud. A second later we were both jumping up and down on it in our cowboy boots. It was true that the wood felt a little squishy underfoot, the angle irons bending ominously under our collective weight. But then again, neither of us put a foot through it.

"I don't know," Joe said. "It might work."

"Let's put him in and find out."

I grabbed a halter and led Red up to the trailer. He stopped just short of the ramp, sticking out a front hoof to test it.

"He's never gone up a ramp before," I said. "He'll get the idea in a minute."

Three times I led the horse up to the ramp, urging him forward with little slaps on his butt with the end of the lead rope. On the third try, he walked right up the ramp. The angle irons groaned and the wood gave off a cracking sound, but soon enough Red was standing on the solid planks of the trailer floor.

"Told you it would hold," I announced with triumph.

"Yeah, but will it close?" Joe asked. "Look at how far Red's butt sticks out. I'm telling you, that's one long horse."

I stepped back to take a look. Red's chest was tight against the padded front bar of the trailer, and yet his hindquarters stuck out the back a good five or six inches. Still, there was nothing for it but to try. Lifting the ramp with a groan, I leaned into it with my shoulder until I could drop a cotter key on one side, then moved to the other side and repeated the process. It was like forcing your foot into a shoe that's a couple of sizes too small.

"Wow, that's tight," Joe observed. "And there's no butt-bar to lock him in there. What if he leans all twelve hundred pounds of himself against that ramp?"

An image entered my mind unbidden: Red flying backwards out of the trailer while I was doing 70 mph on I-70.

"If he were only five or six inches shorter," Joe began.

"I know, I know," I said, raising a hand to interrupt him. "You don't have to rub it in. It's pretty clear what's happened here. I just paid a thousand bucks for a trailer that's too short to haul my goddamn horse!"

Joe stood there, shrugging in a manner that said, *Tough luck, but it is what it is.*

The following day, as I made the return trip to Indianapolis, I considered the deep irony of animal husbandry. So far, counting the running lights, I'd dropped $1,500 on the trailer and another $300 on Red's stall, to say nothing of all the gas I was burning ($200 at last count!).

So I'm already two grand into this deal, I shook my head ruefully, *and I still have to buy hay and grain and somehow get Red to Indy.*

It was then I remembered the alfalfa bales Joe had stowed in the front of the trailer. Bales of that kind sold for $4 or $5 apiece. What had I paid, though, when you factored in all the gas I was burning driving to and from Kansas City? A hundred dollars a bale, maybe? A hundred and twenty-five?

Before I went to bed that night, I took a picture of the black trailer and posted it on craigslist. *FOR SALE: LIGHT, EASY-TO-PULL, EURO-STYLE HORSE TRAILER. $1,500 OBO.*

A week later, I unloaded the thing for $950 to the first buyer who came along, an eager, middle-aged fellow driving a $50,000 SUV.

"My wife said I wouldn't find a trailer for under a grand," he laughed as I took his money. "I guess I showed her."

"Oh, you showed her, all right," I said.

A week later, the trailer was back on craigslist, priced this time at an even $1,000.

I didn't bother buying another trailer. Instead, I took half the money from the sale of the black one and paid to have Red shipped to Indianapolis. Shipping a horse is a curious business involving not a few hidden expenses, for example, paying to have blood work done to prove that your horse is free of Equine Infectious Anemia, among other diseases. However, it's far cheaper than buying a trailer and hauling the horse yourself, especially if you have no long-term need of a trailer. In fact, the only real downside to shipping a horse is the timing. It's not like shipping a package UPS or driving to the airport to meet someone's flight. Instead, you're given a one- or two-day window when the horse might show up, depending on a number of factors outside of your control, including the destinations of the other horses on the trailer, the route chosen by the driver, and, trickiest of all, the weather. From the time the horse is loaded onto the transporter until he's finally delivered, several days later, you're basically on call.

Red was picked up in Kansas City on the evening of July 2. Had the driver brought him straight to Indy, he'd have arrived early the following morning. But that's not close to what happened. Instead, the driver got only as far as St. Louis before he "stashed" Red at a farm west of the city and headed north into Iowa to pick up another horse. ("I just go where the dispatcher tells me to go," the driver later confided to me in his backwoods accent. "They was plenty of room on the trailer, but I just figured, why in hail should Big Red have to go to Ioway? He ain't got no business up there.") The driver lay over near Cedar Rapids until the afternoon of July 3 ("Too hot to haul hosses in the middle of the day"), then headed south for Kentucky, picking up Red along the way. I know all of this because I kept calling the dispatcher in Dallas to ask when I could expect my horse. "Don't worry, honey," she kept telling me. "The driver will call you when he gets close. For now, just sit tight and enjoy your holiday."

I did my best to take this advice. On the afternoon of July 4, we were invited to a pool party at a neighbor's house. I went to the party but took my phone with me and kept checking it the whole time I was there.

"Expecting a call?" my neighbor asked.

"I'm expecting a *horse*," I answered. "He should have been here a day ago, but it seems there's no telling when he might show up."

Hours later there was still no word on Red. Darkness fell over the neighborhood. I began to calculate how long it would have taken me to ride the horse from Kansas City. Meanwhile, fireworks began to fill up the sky over downtown Indy. I sat on my patio, cell phone in my lap, wondering where Red could be at that moment. Tennessee? Florida? Central America?

Then, a little after ten o'clock, the phone buzzed in my lap.

"Howdy, is this Mr. Rib? . . . Reeb? . . . "

"Ray-bine, yes. Are you the driver?"

"Yessir, I'm about ten minutes from your place right now. Is there a driveway, or do you wanna unload him out on the road?"

"There's a driveway, but don't pull in there," I said. "It's against barn rules."

Alyssa and I jumped into her Passat and headed for the barn. From half a mile away, we could see the red taillights of the transporter stopped in the middle of the road. The driver was redirecting traffic with a flashlight. When we pulled up, he tried to redirect us, too.

"That's my horse you've got on there," I said, at which point he stuck his entire head through Alyssa's window and said, "Whooee, it's hotter than two billy goats making love in a wool sock. How y'all doing, anyway?"

"Great," I said. "Now that you're here."

"That's one big-ass hoss you got. Should I pull him out, or do you wanna do it?"

"I'll do it."

Fireworks were going off in the sky overhead. The driver pulled a pair of horses out of the back of the trailer and I stepped in among the woodchips and hay and untied Red's lead rope, which I recognized immediately from the tack room on my family's ranch in Kansas. I was almost as glad to see this tiny piece of my Kansas world as I was to see the horse, whose shoes made a clicking sound as I unloaded him onto the paved road. By now, there were three or four cars waiting in the road behind Alyssa's VW. I quickly signed the driver's paperwork ("Call me if you ever need him moved again; we go anywhere but Alaska and Hawaii!") and led Red across a grassy ditch into the front yard of the co-op. As I came up out of the ditch, a Roman candle exploded just above our heads—*kaboom!*—and Red took a big leap sideways, landing on my booted foot.

"Son of a bitch!" I spat out. It was all I could do to hang onto the lead rope as the frightened animal took several more sideways leaps. "Easy now, big boy. Easy." Finally the horse calmed down enough that I was able to lead him toward the barn, limping the whole way.

Days before, in anticipation of Red's arrival, Alyssa and I had lined his stall with a thick blanket of wood chips and sawdust. He entered the stall willingly, eager to get away from the fireworks, which continued to explode in the sky above the open door of the barn. After he was safely inside, we topped off his water and hay and stood a while before the bars of his stall, watching him eat.

"Well, he's finally here," Alyssa said. "Are you happy?"

"I don't know. Relieved might be a better word."

But even as I said this, another part of me was filling up with cautious excitement at all that was unfolding. Before me in his tidy stall was a horse that had been born and raised on the plains of western Kansas, just as I had been. But now, through an act of audacious dreaming, here he was in Indiana. Was this genius or folly?

Only time would tell.

The owner of the barn had informed me that I'd need to "tag along" with a barn regular named Stephanie for my first couple of feedings. When I pulled into the gravel driveway a little after 6:30 a.m., a rusted-out Buick was already parked by the side door, and Stephanie, a tall, blonde woman in her late twenties, was leaning against the driver's side door sipping from a cup of gas station coffee. She gave me a slow, exaggerated wave as I came up, the gravel of the driveway crunching beneath my boots.

"Hello. You must be Robert. I was just looking at your horse. Very flashy. Are you gonna show him?"

"I don't know," I said. "I don't think so."

"Well, you should. Eileen tells me you've got a couple of kids."

Eileen was the barn owner. "I do," I answered, wondering what she was getting at with her questions. "But I don't see them showing, either."

"Too bad. Is that all your hay in the far back stall?"

I nodded. In the days before I sold the black trailer, I'd used it to haul forty bales of alfalfa from a farm a few miles away.

"How much did you pay?"

"Five dollars a bale."

"A little steep," Stephanie said, sipping her coffee. "But you'll be very glad you have it when winter kicks in and everyone else is scrambling. Come on. I'll show you how Eileen likes things done."

I followed her through the tiny room where grain was stored and from there into the dark, shadow-cast barn.

"It's a pretty simple operation during the summer," she said. "Most people keep their horses outside all the time, so there's not much cleanup. In the winter, things get a little more complicated."

All of the stall doors stood open except for four at the back of the barn. In the stall closest to the back was Red, who'd been confined for the past two days while the other horses got used to him. In the stall next to him was the Shetland pony and her nursing colt. Finally, there were two more stalls where a couple of older geldings, a black and a brown, paced and nickered in anticipation of breakfast.

"Why are those horses kept inside at night, when all of the others are left outside?" I asked.

"Because those are Jim's horses," Stephanie said, rolling her eyes. "Have you met Jim?" I shook my head. "Nice guy, and he certainly pulls his weight around here in terms of barn chores. But he and his wife know nothing at all about horses. Neither of them rides. Pet owners is what they are. Why don't you grab that big race horse and lead him out of here, and I'll see about the ponies."

We led the horses, one by one, from the barn to the lots outside. Then we loaded hay from each owner's stack into wheelbarrows and hauled it to where the horses waited in frantic anticipation. The wildest were the horses in the far back pasture: Stephanie's tall, white jumper, a couple of Arabian mares owned by Eileen, and an old quarter horse owned by Eileen's son, who lived in the house with the ski boat. The whole time I was feeding Red, these horses raced up and down the fence line separating us from them, heads held high, tails raised behind them. When they ran up against the fence corner, they planted their front feet and slid to a stop, then pivoted on their hindquarters and thundered off in the opposite direction.

"Yeah, yeah, yeah," Stephanie said. "We'll get to you all in a minute."

While the horses were eating, we dragged hoses to their water troughs and filled them one by one. Mosquitoes buzzed in the air around my face and neck. It was only a quarter past seven in the morning, but already I could feel the heat of the day coming on. The watering done, I rolled up the hose, then joined Stephanie in the grain room, where she was using a measuring cup to scoop sweet feed into each horse's bucket. These we hauled out to where the horses were finishing up their hay and stood watching for the two or three minutes it took for each horse to devour the grain.

"All right," Stephanie said. "Fun part's over. Time to clean Mr. Pet Owner's stalls."

We emptied the water buckets and proceeded to muck the stalls, shoveling manure and wet bedding into wheelbarrows. When a wheelbarrow got to be a third or so full, we'd wheel it outside and push it up a short ramp and into the manure trailer.

"What happens when the trailer gets full?" I asked.

"That hardly ever happens," Stephanie said. "A couple of nights a week, an old hippie comes out and hooks the trailer to his car and hauls it to some organic farm. It's the only part of this whole operation that works the way it's supposed to."

There was an edge of wry complaint to everything Stephanie said, good-natured but sharp-tongued as well, as if to say, *I will joke my way through all this, but I won't pretend to enjoy it. Why should I?*

"What about you?" I asked, picking up an earlier thread in our conversation. "Do you show your horse?"

"I used to," she said. "Now I'm trying to finish up a degree I've been working on for far too long. I've got a boyfriend and a job I work three nights a week. Plus I live about twenty miles south of here, in Greenwood."

"Greenwood!" I said. "Why not choose a barn closer to where you live?"

"Can't afford to," she shrugged. "Hell, I can't afford this barn. I can't afford the fucking gas it's costing me to get out here four times a week. It's just that I know Eileen through horses, and she lets me work some of my bill down every month."

"So why do it?" I asked. "Why not just sell the horse and be done with the whole mess?"

"Ah, the voice of reason," Stephanie laughed. "Sure, I've got that voice in my head. But I've also got this other voice, the one that keeps saying, 'If you sell that horse, you'll be nothing but a tired waitress with thirty grand in student loan debt.' So that's me. That's where I'm at currently."

We gathered rakes and wheelbarrows and put them away in the empty stall where all the mucking equipment was kept. I consulted my watch. From start to finish, the chores that morning had taken just under an hour.

"Think you've got the hang of it?" Stephanie asked as she climbed into her beat-up Buick.

"Yeah, I've got it," I said. "No need for you to come out for my next feeding. I can handle it fine by myself."

"That's sweet of you," she said, starting the car. "But don't tell Eileen."

"I won't," I promised.

I stood and watched as she rolled out of there, a thin cloud of white smoke coming from the Buick's tailpipe.

We settled into the rhythms and routines of animal husbandry. Three or four times a week, the kids and I, or Alyssa and I, or sometimes the family as a whole, would drive the seven miles to the barn. It was summer, and both kids had plenty of time to help with barn chores. Even the most mundane task, like stacking hay or harrowing the indoor arena with an old riding mower, was new and exciting to them. Watching them perform these chores, I'd joke that maybe they weren't "one hundred percent city kids" after all. Maybe they had some ranch kid in them, too—a sixteenth of their total being, say, or maybe it was an eighth.

"Come on, Dad," Jake would fire back. "We've got more ranch kid in us than that."

I was only teasing, and yet there was some truth in the observation. No matter how many hours they spent riding or mucking stalls, they'd never have the sort of childhood I'd experienced in Kansas thirty years before. They'd never work cattle at age ten, drive a tractor at twelve, run a load of wheat to the co-op elevator at fifteen or sixteen. Of course, while achieving these rural milestones, I'd missed out on any number of other experiences: swimming lessons, summer camp, playing organized baseball past the age of eleven or twelve. A thought began to pop up in my brain: Maybe having Red in the picture would allow Ria and Jake to experience the best of both worlds. Maybe, unlike me, they'd never feel split between two separate identities. It was a little strange to know, as I went about my life in the city, that I also had a shadow life in the country that called for a different wardrobe (barn coat, muck boots, work gloves) and that took me to different places (feed store, large animal vet) than I otherwise would have frequented. It was as though I were living two lives simultaneously—the life I'd chosen when I left Dodge City to attend college, and the life I might have known had I stayed in Kansas and become a farmer or rancher. Was that what Joe was up to in Kansas City with his string of horses and his barn full of freshly cut hay? Suddenly, without even trying to, I felt like I understood my brother much better.

After months of scheming and several thousand dollars in horse-related expenses, we were finally set up to ride. It went without saying that taking turns riding in a barn or a two-acre pasture wasn't what we were used to from family trips to Kansas, where everyone got his own horse and the open plains stretched off for miles in every direction. But it was still riding for all that. In fact, it was precisely the sort of riding Red had been born and bred to do. Years on the show circuit, followed by several semesters as a lesson horse at the community college, had turned him into a highly calibrated machine. He could side pass, roll back, slide to a stop, and spin. "Hell, there's more buttons on that horse than you'll ever know how to push," Dave McCollum, the trainer at the community college, had told me over the phone. At the time I'd thought he was exaggerating, but I could see now that it was true. The first time I asked Red to canter, he settled into the slowest, smoothest "rocking-horse" lope you could imagine. He covered ground, yes, but you could've sipped a cup of Starbucks up there and not spilled a drop.

All of the best times at the barn took place that summer and fall, when chores were minimal and we had a lot of extra time in our schedules. Three or four times a week, we'd drop whatever we were doing in the city and head out to the country to ride. Often the kids would invite friends from the neighborhood to come along. It provided the perfect opportunity to show off the reining patterns I'd been teaching them.

"Oh my God, I love this horse!" Ria would shout, beaming down at where her two best friends stood waiting their turn in their tennis shoes and shorts.

"Wait until the next time you're on the ranch," I'd say. "Your cousins won't believe how much you've improved."

Maybe it was a little strange to keep comparing everything to the ranch, but I couldn't help it. Every time I saw Red hitting that rocking-horse lope, my parents' ranch on the Sawlog in western Kansas was the first thing that came to mind.

Then autumn arrived, and the tempo of our lives began to change. The days grew shorter, and time in the family schedule grew more scarce. Football practice started, followed by school proper. Ria and Jake were getting up at 6:00 a.m., scarfing down breakfast, and heading off into a busy day that didn't end until 6:30 or 7:00 p.m., and usually there was an hour or more of homework to do after that. Luckily, Ria's kickball practice got out at 4:30 p.m. A couple of days a week, I'd pick her up after practice and we'd make a mad dash into the country to get some riding in before we had to hurry back into town to pick up Jake from football. That was on afternoons when I had no barn chores in the evening. On days when I was scheduled to feed, I preferred to go to the barn later—at 7:30 or 8:00. Sometimes Alyssa or Jake would go with me, but more often I went by myself. There was so much going on—homework, cooking dinner, packing bags for the day to come—that it was hard to justify pulling Alyssa or the kids away from these tasks just so I'd have company feeding horses.

"The horses are your company," Alyssa would joke.

And so they were. Moving horses from stall to stall, I'd usually engage in what horse people call "groundwork," asking each horse to bend his neck, back up, circle to the right or left. Groundwork was not riding, but it had many similarities to riding, and there was pleasure to be taken in it. It was like dancing, in a way. There was that same careful coordination of movement, the picking up of a foot here in order to put it down there, each of these movements agreed upon with the lightest of touches, the merest of suggestions. There was pleasure, too, in grooming a horse—running a comb through mane or tail, picking up a foot to scrape mud from a hoof wall. Even cleaning stalls could be enjoyable provided the weather was fine—one of those autumn days when the air is crisp and the earth feels bountiful and ripe.

I remember one evening, having finished feeding and watering horses, I walked out into the back pasture and stood watching as a combine harvester cut soybeans in an adjacent field. The sounds and smells of harvest—the steady clank of the sickle as it cut through stalks, the smell of chaff rising into the air—these were things freighted with memory and deep associations with my childhood. But even as I noted the similarities, another part of me was busy cataloging all of the differences. The combine cutting the beans was small compared to those used in Kansas; the field of beans (also small) was next to a subdivision full of beige boxes, and so on.

One day, late in that fall season, we traveled to the barn to take our annual Christmas picture. There are four faces in that picture, which I keep framed on the desk where I work: daughter, son, beagle, horse. The autumn light is thin and soft, Ria and Jake are smiling, the halter strap running across Red's nose bears the words *I (HEART) MY HORSE*. In the background, though, everything is yellow and the trees are almost completely devoid of leaves. Looking at it now, I see that the picture records a moment of transition, of one reality passing away and another looming.

Shortly after the picture was taken, football season ended and practices for winter sports started up. As in years past, I volunteered to coach Ria's basketball team as well as Jake's wrestling team. These were large commitments, but combined with our feeding and riding schedules, they loomed even larger. From Halloween until spring break, with a couple of weeks off for Christmas, I'd be coaching every afternoon or evening, with games and meets thrown into the mix most weekends. It was this annual coaching commitment that had always given me the most pause whenever Alyssa and I discussed moving to the country or buying a horse. How would I manage to juggle practice and barn duties and still keep up with things at work and home? It was a daunting prospect, to be sure.

Then, with winter coming on, both of the barn owner's granddaughters abruptly sold their horses and dropped out of the feeding rotation. Since the barn owner herself had relocated to Las Vegas for the winter, that left only three of us—Stephanie, Mr. Pet Owner, and me—to divide up all of the feeding and stall-cleaning duties. Instead of having three feedings a week to cover, suddenly I was on the hook for five: two evening shifts, which I fit in after wrestling practice, and three in the early morning hours before work and school.

Meanwhile, new directives had come down from Vegas via text message.

> Getting COLD!!!! ALL of the
> horses need to be kept IN
> at night. It's A LOT more
> work, but don't get SLOPPY!!!

Clean the ENTIRE stall EVERY
TIME!!!!

Reading this text, which I imagined having been composed pool-side, cocktail resting on a nearby table, made me want to set all of the horses loose on the road before heading back into town, never to return.

Sometimes, at the beginning or end of barn chores, I'd run into Stephanie or Mr. Pet Owner, and we'd stand around berating our absentee barn owner or commiserating about the many hardships of animal husbandry. It was during one of these bitch sessions that Stephanie let it drop that her days at the barn were numbered.

"I just don't know how much longer I can keep it up," she said. "I was okay with three feedings a week, but coming out here five times is killing me. The gas alone—"

"Stop right there," I said. "You can't do this to me, not now."

"Yeah, well, that's not all."

I took note of the dark circles under her eyes and the way she fidg-eted around, not knowing what to do with her hands. "What?"

"I'm pregnant," she announced flatly.

"No."

"Yes. Yes, I'm afraid I am."

I stood there in silence, letting the news sink in. I'd always been one of the lucky ones when it came to announcements of pregnancy. Both times had been moments of great anticipation and joy. But not now.

"So what are you gonna do?"

"Get rid of my horse, obviously," she answered. "Problem is, it's the wrong time of year, and the market is really down right now. I prob-ably couldn't give him away, not with winter coming on."

Having said this, she gave me a studied, sorrowful look—deep frown on her face, eyes bright with pleading.

"No way," I said. "I'm in over my head as it is."

I did, however, promise to cover for her if the weather got bad

enough that making the drive from Greenwood in her old Buick became too difficult or treacherous.

"You're a prince," she said.

I felt more like a fool.

Winter was not so bad at first. We had some rain and a few dustings of
snow in early December, but that was it, and life at the barn continued
as before. Then, a couple of weeks before Christmas, eight inches of
snow fell in a single night. The next morning I found the entire north
side of the barn covered in a massive drift. It took half an hour just
to dig my way inside, where I found the horses pacing in their stalls
amid great mounds of manure. Evidently Stephanie had not been able
to make it out from Greenwood the night before. *My God,* I thought.
*I'm the only thing standing between these horses and starvation. If I ever
stopped showing up, they'd die for sure.*

It got worse. In January, after days of rain, the worst ice storm in
a decade swept across central Indiana. Overnight, the city of Indianapolis was turned into a gigantic skating rink, as a sheet of ice more
than an inch thick covered everything—porches, patios, sidewalks,
parking lots, roads. Schools across the city shut down. Government
shut down. There were stories on the radio and TV of people who'd
tried to make it into work, only to land in the ER with a broken wrist
or tailbone.

I was standing in my kitchen looking out at the wreckage when
the text I'd been expecting since late the night before appeared on my
phone.

> Steph is ICED IN!!!!
> Do u think u can make
> it to the barn????
> Bring a hammer or spade
> something to break the ice
> PLEASE!!!!

I climbed into my Jeep and slid backwards down my driveway, narrowly missing a telephone pole, and began the slow trek out to the barn. The main roads had been heavily salted the night before, but the secondary roads were in terrible shape. The only way to stay out of the ditch was to creep along in the dead center of the road at two or three miles an hour. In this way, I finally made it out to the barn. It was the same there as it was in town. Every square inch of the place was encased in a thick sheet of ice. I spent ten minutes chipping at the doorknob on the north side of the barn, hoping to clear enough ice to insert my key. Nothing doing. It would've taken a blowtorch to get in that door. Finally, I gave up trying and concentrated on clearing ice from the rails on which the big barn doors slid. After an hour of chipping—an hour!—I was able to push the doors far enough apart to squeeze between them sideways.

In the barn, the horses were pacing in their stalls as usual. They did not know, nor did they care, that an ice storm had paralyzed the city. All they cared about was hay and grain and fresh water for their buckets. As I fed them, I thought about how long the glacier-like conditions were likely to continue. From what I'd seen, it would take a heat wave—temperatures in the 40s or 50s for a couple of days running—to melt all that ice. And until that happened, none of the horses would be safe outside the barn. They were on lockdown—no different than inmates in a prison where a riot has occurred.

As soon as I was finished mucking out the stalls, I pulled Red out and rode him bareback in the cramped barn, walking him at first, then trotting, then loping him in that wonderful rocking-horse gait he had. "What a splendid beast you are," I said to him as we loped. "And what a shame you're stuck in here with me instead of running across a high pasture or training for your next horse show. But I guess that's just your life, isn't it, just as it's my life to shovel shit from your stall and feed you day and night and protect you from that world of ice outside."

After ten minutes of loping in one direction, I turned Red around and exercised him in the opposite direction. Finished, I pulled Stephanie's big white Standardbred out of his stall and rode him, too. Barn rules forbade riding another co-op member's horse, but I didn't care. I was far beyond barn rules now. The other horses, I exercised on foot—groundwork—twenty or thirty minutes each. It wasn't much, but it was all I could do with work and other responsibilities looming.

For more than a week, as the massive ice sheet continued its grip on the city, I returned to the barn day after day to feed and exercise the horses. The thought of them stuck in their stalls all day and night haunted me. I was spending six or seven hours a day at the barn, far more than I spent at work or coaching. And even when I wasn't at the barn in a physical sense, I was thinking about it—worrying that Mr. Pet Owner would forget to drain the water hose or that the stack of alfalfa I'd put up that summer would run out before the weather broke. I lay awake at night, my body sore from a thousand exertions, contemplating the many things that had gone wrong already, imagining a thousand others that might go wrong. What if the power failed? Did the barn owner have a generator? How would we draw water from the well? Somewhere along the way, the shadow life I'd built for myself in the country had overtaken my real life. I was experiencing the same worries and pressures my rancher father had contended with his whole life. A part of me reveled in the comparison—or at least in the manifold ironies it gave rise to—but another, larger part of me just wanted my old life back with all of its comforts and predictability.

Four or five days into the ice storm, I was standing in the middle of the floodlit barn checking e-mail on my phone while simultaneously exercising the second of six horses I had to put through their paces that morning, when the thought occurred to me. *I can put an end to this whole deal anytime I want. All I have to do is dial the number of that dispatcher in Dallas, and a few days later the same gap-toothed driver who delivered Red will come rolling up the road in his truck and trailer, and it'll be, "Adios, animal husbandry."*

I thumbed through the stored calls on my phone until I came to the dispatcher's number. It thrilled me, in a cheap sort of way, to see that Dallas area code glowing on the screen. There it was—my 911, my "I'm bailing and getting my life back" number.

What the hell, I thought, dialing.

"Hello," came a familiar, scratchy voice. "Do you have an order, or do you need to make one?"

I said nothing. Why talk when what I really needed was to hear her voice?

"Sir? Can I help you? Sir?"

"Yes," I said finally. "You can help. Maybe not today, but one of these days."

I trailed off, standing there in the fractured light of the barn, listening to the woman drag from a cigarette.

"That'll be fine, honey," she said. "You just call me whenever you need to, okay?"

"Yes, I'll do that," I said.

I put the phone in the pocket of my barn coat and stepped forward so that the horse I was exercising rolled back and began to circle me in the opposite direction. In the past minute or so—ever since the woman had uttered the words "Can I help you?"—I'd felt a strange calm descending over me, and I knew that my days of keeping a horse were numbered. I wouldn't bail in the middle of winter, of course. That wouldn't go over so well in Kansas, to say nothing of where it would leave Stephanie and Mr. Pet Owner. Besides, what was the point of keeping a horse all winter if I couldn't ride him a time or two in the spring?

"A time or two," I said over my shoulder to where Red stood sleeping in his stall. "After that, you're out of here."

And so it happened that in late May of that year, roughly ten months after the adventure began, I loaded Red into a rented trailer and hauled him across Indiana and half of Illinois in order to meet up with Joe and some of his trail riding friends in Shawnee National Forest. On the way south, I thought about the abiding ironies of animal husbandry—how hard it was, what a commitment of time and money it entailed, how it threw the seasons and weather itself smack into your face in a way that was rare to experience in the course of a normal city life. I was finished with all that for now. When the weekend was over, I'd load Red into Joe's four-horse trailer to be taken back to Kansas, and I'd be back to my horseless cowboy ways.

But not forever.

One day, I knew, under different circumstances, I'd give horse ownership another shot. When the kids were out of high school, maybe before, Alyssa and I would buy a house in the country where I could walk out my back door and there the horses would be, no driving for miles on iffy roads to get to them, no feeding and mucking stalls without the pleasure of riding. Instead of the two lives that competed with each other inside of me, there'd be just one. My life. The one I'd always wanted.

—11—
Driver's Education

A few years back, I took my fifteen-year-old daughter to a branch office of the Indiana Bureau of Motor Vehicles to get her a learner's permit. All summer long she had pecked away at a 30-unit online driver's education course, fighting off sleep as a bald-headed man named Mike droned on about the "rules of the road." Now the payoff was almost in sight. Having passed the written exam on a previous visit, all that remained was for Ria to pass an eye test and submit proof of residency and citizenship and, bingo, she'd be a licensed driver. The prospect of this happening excited me in a vicarious sort of way, and I found myself soaking in all of the details of the moment: the way the woman sitting across the desk from us checked and rechecked all of the documents, the care she took to explain that federal law forbade Ria from smiling in her official license photo, and so on. These were details worth remembering forever—or at least that's the way I felt about them. When I turned to Ria to get her reaction, I found her hunched over the screen of her cell phone, thumbs moving rapidly.

"Put that thing away," I said, irritated. "We're here to get your license, not to text with your friends."

"It's the volleyball girls," Ria responded, still texting away. "They're talking about the club season. Important stuff."

"Well, this is important, too," I said. "You're here with me, not them, and I've taken time out of my day—"

"Okay, okay," she said, shutting the phone off and slipping it under the waistband of her running shorts. "I'm back. Let's do this thing."

This lack of interest in learning to drive—indeed, in external reality itself—was something I'd been noticing for a while. It bothered me on a couple of levels. Sure, I had a cell phone to which I gave more attention than it deserved. But did I have the thing out right then and there? Was I checking my messages instead of participating in an important rite of passage in my child's burgeoning adolescence? No, I was not.

For days afterward, I found myself returning to the episode, turning it over in my mind, talking about it with Ria's mom at bedtime, venting about it with coworkers around the proverbial water cooler.

"My God," I said, shaking my head. "When I was that age, I couldn't *wait* to start driving."

"Different eras," one coworker observed.

"Personally, I'm glad my son doesn't want to drive," another chuckled. "That's all the world needs—another exhaust pipe."

"Wasn't there a piece about this in the *New York Times*?" a third asked. "Something about Millennials preferring iPhones to cars? Like if you said to them, 'It's either your phone or your car,' they'd choose the phone?"

"Please don't call them 'Millennials,'" I said irritably. "Do you want people referring to you as a 'Gen-Xer'?"

"Well, I'm pretty sure that's what the article said. Phones over cars. I mean, it makes no sense to *us*, but. . . . "

Back at my computer, I typed "teenagers prefer iPhone to cars" into Google, and the article in question popped right up, along with a more recent piece from the *Los Angeles Times*. The statistics quoted by these newspapers astounded me. In 1983, 69 percent of seventeen-year-olds had driver's licenses, compared with just 46 percent in 2010 (*LA Times*). Forty-six percent of Americans ages eighteen to twenty-four would choose access to the Internet over access to a car of their own (*NYT*).

My God, I thought, beginning to feel actual despair. *How on earth can this be?*

According to Sheryl Connelly, a Ford Motor Company executive quoted in the *New York Times* piece, the reason was simple. "The car used to be the signal of adulthood, of freedom," Connelly said. Today, by contrast, the act of driving is seen not as a symbol of freedom but as limiting "the valuable time teenagers could use to text-message with their friends or update their social networks." An auto industry analyst named Thilo Koslowski put the matter more bluntly still: "The iPhone is the Ford Mustang of today."

I thought of a biography of Apple founder Steve Jobs I'd been reading. Jobs's father, Paul, was a dyed-in-the-wool motorhead, obsessively building and rebuilding muscle cars in the family garage in Los Altos, California. Young Steve, preferring electronics to cars, chose a different path—and in the process changed the world forever.

Things were very different when I was growing up in western Kansas in the 1970s and early '80s. The son of a farmer and rancher, I learned to drive at eleven or twelve and got my first driver's license the summer I turned fourteen. No one had to prod me or pave the way for this to happen. Like all of my friends, boys and girls alike, I couldn't wait to start driving, to get my first license, to buy my first car.

I vividly recall the day I got my license. As a farm kid, I never lacked for opportunities to drive. By the time I was thirteen, I had operated everything from three-quarter-ton pickups to four-wheel-drive tractors to diesel-powered grain trucks. What I didn't have was the time—or the need, according to my father—to go through the process of getting an actual license.

"What's the point?" my father would ask every time I raised the subject. "It's not like you're getting ready to drive to Wichita or somewhere else where they don't know you."

The way he saw things, driving a car was a simple if learned act, like swimming or riding a bicycle. Getting a license was a mere formality. Budding teenager that I was, I knew that he was wrong about this and that getting a license (and after that a car) was nothing less than a declaration of independence. It was not the wheat fields and dirt roads where my father toiled on a daily basis that I wanted to explore, but rather the streets—and back streets—of town. I wanted to roll up to the Sonic on Wyatt Earp Boulevard and order a cherry Coke. I wanted to cruise through Wright Park with my windows rolled down and my stereo blasting Dire Straits. I wanted to sit on the hood of a muscle car talking to girls while the sun dropped over the riverbank behind us.

And so I kept after my father, bringing up the business of the license day after day throughout the summer I turned fourteen, until finally, during a spell of rainy weather, he acquiesced and let me drive one of the farm pickups into town to take the test. "Go straight there, ask to take the written test, and if you pass that, take the driving test, too," he said, treating the matter like it was some kind of errand he was having me run, like going to the John Deere dealership to pick up a new sickle blade for the combine.

The license bureau was a squat brick building on the east side of town. A couple of women in bouffant hairdos and cat eye glasses administered written tests and gave vision exams, while a stout man in a blue highway patrolman's uniform sat behind a third desk, reading a newspaper. I spent an hour studying a little booklet one of the bouffant ladies gave me, then sat in a desk chair and took the written part of the exam, which consisted of a hundred or so questions taken directly from the study booklet. I remember watching anxiously as one of the women marked my exam. It seemed to me that I would fail for sure given the ferocity with which she circled each of my wrong answers. But, lo and behold, I passed, causing the man in the patrolman's uniform to fold his newspaper and rise out of his chair.

"You brought a vehicle with you, I take it?"

"Yes."

"All right, then. Lead the way."

We walked out into the blinding sunlight, the patrolman putting on a pair of aviator shades that made him look far more serious and cool than he had seemed inside. We climbed into the cab of my father's Silverado, the patrolman struggling to find and then to fasten his seat belt.

"Don't look to me like these belts have been used much," the man observed. "Never, would be my guess. Still, you'd best put yours on. It's part of the test."

I did as I was told, and soon we were tooling through the streets of east Dodge City, headed for Wyatt Earp Boulevard. I performed every action requested of me with the utmost attention to detail. I checked my rearview mirror every few seconds, and I don't think my hands left the ten o'clock and two o'clock positions once during the whole drive.

"Pull in here," the patrolman said as Daylight Donuts came up on our right. "Okay. Now park." Again, I did as I was told, watching through the glass windows of the donut shop as the patrolman went inside to buy himself a bear claw and a cup of coffee. "All right," he said as he settled back into his seat in the Silverado. "Make a left here and let's head back."

In the parking lot of the license bureau, he asked if I ever had occasion to ride a motorcycle. I told him I did. "Well then, we might as well put an *M* on here, too, to go along with your *C*," he announced as he checked a series of boxes on his clipboard. "No sense in you coming down here twice."

"Does that mean . . . I passed?" I asked nervously.

This brought a chuckle and a shake of the head. "You farm kids really crack me up, you know that? Hell, *yes*, you passed."

The license that came in the mail a few days later was made of paper and featured no picture on the front, just a brief description (green eyes, five-eleven, 145 pounds), but I considered it to be—and it was—my ticket to the world. Days after getting it, I was cruising up and down Wyatt Earp Boulevard in my mother's Buick La Sabre with my friends Jeff and Kent Green. "We're out!" I remember Kent shouting. "No holding us back now!" To emphasize the point, I burned a little rubber at the next stoplight, holding down the gas and the brake pedals simultaneously until a thick cloud of blue-white smoke lifted into the air behind us.

Within six months of getting that license, I had a car of my own—a canary yellow 1974 Mustang II that I bought with the money I'd earned working on the farm. A year after that, I traded the Mustang straight across for my brother Steve's ghost green 1970 Firebird Formula 400, a car he deemed too much of a gas guzzler to take to college. It was his loss. I doubt if an astronaut sitting atop a rocket ship has felt more powerful and soon-to-be-launched than I felt sitting behind the wheel of that Formula 400.

Can it really be true that today's teenagers aspire to none of this, preferring to trade pictures online or dance their thumbs across a glass screen? Apparently it is true. No less of a cultural authority than the *New York Times* has declared it to be so. And yet I still find it hard to believe. To me, an iPhone will always be a poor substitute for a Mustang—let alone a Firebird Formula 400.

But maybe there's hope after all.

A few weeks after she got her learner's permit, my daughter and I began making entries in her official Log of Supervised Driving Practice. In Indiana, state law requires teen drivers to log fifty such hours—ten of them at night—before they are set loose on the road by themselves. At first Ria seemed reluctant to begin even this supervised form of driving. I had to prod and remind her, the same way I had to prod and remind her younger brother to take out the trash and brush his teeth. "All right, all right," she'd say, rolling her eyes. It was almost as though I were the teenager dying to get my first license, and she was my rancher father, consumed by other things and failing to see the point of it all.

We started small, tooling around the newly paved parking lot of a church near our house. From there, we moved on to wide residential streets with few obstacles to negotiate. Finally we tackled the busier two-lane roads of the city with their dedicated turn lanes and stoplights and pedestrian crossings. It all came so easily to Ria. She'd always been a fast learner, always had a certain calm about her that belied her years.

"You're a natural," I declared after a few of these sessions. "It's like driving is in your blood or something."

"Thanks," she said, smiling at the compliment.

A few days after this, Ria and I were invited to a party at a friend's house a half hour away. It was a mixed party, adults in the kitchen and sprawling back patio, kids in the basement. Fifteen or twenty of her high school cronies were going to be there, including two girls who lived near us who had texted Ria to ask if they could catch a ride. "Sure," I said, as we headed for where my wife's Volkswagen Passat sat parked in the driveway.

"I'll drive," Ria said, cutting in front of me and holding out a hand for the keys.

"Are you sure?" I asked. "We haven't practiced driving at night."

"Dad, it's no problem," she said.

I handed her the keys, smiling inwardly.

We pulled up in front of a house a block from ours, and Ria's friend Lea came running across the front lawn, only to stop and do a double take when she saw Ria behind the wheel.

"Ria! *You're* driving!"

Ria nodded, the epitome of cool.

The same scene repeated itself at another house a few blocks away, as Ria's friend Lauren climbed into the back seat next to Lea and let out an exaggerated "Oh my God, we're all gonna die!"

We hung a left onto busy Washington Street, the old National Road. Ria reached forward and turned on the radio. As we cruised past strip malls and fast-food joints on the way to the party, Ria and her friends talked and laughed and ribbed each other, shrieking whenever a song they liked came on the radio. "Turn it up! Turn it up!"

I sat quietly in the passenger's seat, memories of my own teen years washing over me. *We're out! No holding us back!* It was like I was back in my mother's Buick or, better yet, that ghost green Formula 400, headed to the Sonic or Boot Hill parking lot or some lakeside keg party, the car packed to the gills with friends, Bruce Springsteen's "Born to Run" blasting from the stereo. Hadn't my father and uncles and all of my older brothers done and said these exact same things? Hadn't the same vibe of raucous anticipation reigned supreme? Yes, of course. The cars and the songs had been different, but the essential feeling hadn't changed at all.

When we arrived at the party, a gaggle of teenagers, half of them gangly boys who reminded me of myself at that age, were gathered on the front porch, hands lit up with cell phones. "Check out who's driving!" one of the boys yelled across the lawn. "Lady Ria! You're killing it, girl!"

"You know I am," Ria answered.

A subtle irony, a kind of twenty-first-century cool, pervaded the exchange. The boys expressing shock weren't really shocked. After all, they'd been clued in that Ria was driving almost a half hour before, when Lea and Lauren had texted them about it. And while Ria was justifiably proud of having pulled off the feat, a first among her immediate friends, she wasn't that proud. After all, it wasn't as though driving had the kind of cachet among teenagers that it had enjoyed back in the 1970s and 1980s, let alone the 1950s and 1960s.

Still, you have to take comfort where you find it. On the way up the sidewalk to the party, when Ria tried to hand me the keys, I shrugged and told her I was having none of that. "You're driving, not me," I said.

"Fine," she answered absently, stuffing the keys into the back pocket of her jeans, right next to her iPhone.

—12—
Home on the Range

I tried three different doors before I finally made it into Manor of the Plains, the nursing home where my father had landed following a car wreck that had required separate stints in the ER and critical care units of a hospital in Wichita. I was on foot, having walked to the facility from my parents' sprawling ranch house five blocks away, and I mistakenly tried the doors to the Independent Living and Assisted Living wings before I finally came to Long-Term Care and Skilled Nursing, where I punched a security code into a keypad (the code was prominently displayed above the pad) and stepped through the glass entryway.

I wasn't looking forward to what lay ahead. Two months earlier, visiting my father in the critical care unit in Wichita, I'd found him to be frightened and delusional, prone to uncharacteristic confusion and anger. Among other injuries, he suffered from a broken arm and several broken ribs, and when asked by the trauma doc who the president of the United States was, he answered haltingly, "Damned if I know. Jimmy Carter?" I'd heard from several of my brothers that he was doing better now, but that didn't lessen my anxiety about seeing the hero of my childhood in a place my mother had described over the phone as "an Alzheimer's ward."

The place was busy, with residents in wheelchairs cramming the narrow hallway leading to the nurses' station. Decorations for Halloween were taped to the walls and pinned to bulletin boards. In the cafeteria, a white-haired resident with thick glasses was leading a half dozen others in a sing-along. *Oh she'll be coming around the mountain when she comes. She'll be coming around the mountain when she comes.* Further on, a man in his nineties with a back ravaged by osteoporosis sat slumped forward in his wheelchair next to the nurses' station. "Help me . . . help me . . . help me," the man said.

I passed a room where a couple of physical therapists were helping another man onto a recumbent exercise bike. The man, who looked vaguely familiar, smiled and gave a little wave, causing me to pause at the door.

"How's it going?" I asked.

"Okay," he said, his eyes seeming to laugh at me from behind thick bifocals. "I read your book. It was good, but I only believed about half of it."

"Is that right?" I said with a laugh.

A couple of years earlier, I'd published a memoir that was reviewed on the front page of the local paper. Not many people outside of Kansas knew the book existed, but among townspeople of my parents' generation, I was a minor celebrity.

"You know," I continued, "only about a third of that book is true. So I still got you."

"Ha, I thought so," the man laughed, his thin legs beginning a slow pedal.

I was halfway to my father's room before I was able to put a name with the man's face. Thirty years ago, when I was a teenager planning my escape from the town, he'd been one of its most prominent businessmen—a dashing figure in a top-down Cadillac, ever-present cigarette hanging from his lips. How old could he have been back then? Fifty? Fifty-five? I thought of the E. B. White essay "Once More to the Lake," especially the ending, where a middle-aged White watches his adolescent son pull on a pair of wet swimming trunks and feels "the chill of death" in his groin. I'd just turned fifty myself.

The accident that landed my father in the ER and then in Manor of the Plains occurred at a dangerous highway crossing near the hamlet of Howell, Kansas, six and a half miles west of Dodge City. I know the crossing well, having made it countless times during my teen years, often in overloaded wheat trucks with unreliable brakes. It was a little after eight o'clock in the morning, and according to several eyewitnesses, my father was trying to cross the highway at a place where visibility was notoriously poor. As the central account had it, he'd rolled up to the stop sign on the Howell side of the road, paused briefly, then started across the busy road, apparently without checking to see who was coming in the east or westbound lanes. Halfway across, perhaps sensing the landscaping truck that was bearing down on him, he froze. The truck's driver mashed his brakes and laid on the horn, causing my father to floor it in a desperate attempt to make it across. Instead, he drove directly into the path of the truck, which hit him in the passenger's door before veering into the ditch and taking out a telephone pole. The truck was going perhaps twenty-five miles an hour on impact, and the driver was unhurt. As for my father, it took the Jaws of Life to free him from the wreckage.

Several questions arise from this admittedly sketchy account.

(1) What was my father, an eighty-two-year-old semicripple, doing at the Howell elevator on a Tuesday morning in August?

(2) Did he even look to see the truck bearing down on him, or did the arthritis in his back and neck keep him from turning his head more than an inch or two to check for oncoming traffic?

(3) Did he hear anything before the driver laid on his horn, or did his only partially disguised deafness prevent that?

(4) Finally, why on earth was a man in my father's obviously debilitated condition operating a motor vehicle in the first place?

The answers to these questions depend on whom you ask. Ask my father, and he will tell you: (1) He has no memory at all of the wreck, but was undoubtedly on important business having to do with the farm and ranch he continued to operate to the amazement of his family and friends. (2) If he didn't see the truck, it had nothing to do with his inability to turn his neck; after all, he was still capable of turning *at the waist* to check for oncoming traffic. (3) He hears just fine. (4) None of your goddamned business. Ask anyone else, including my mother or any of my six brothers, and the answers get a tad more complicated. Either that or they lead to more questions. For example, how do you tell a man whose entire life has been defined by his unwillingness to quit in the face of adversity that the time has come to hang it up?

The Friday after the accident, I drove five hundred miles from my home in Indianapolis to Kansas City, continuing on the next day and arriving at the hospital in Wichita around noon. My mother, who had taken up residence in a nearby motel, met me outside my father's room in the critical care unit.

"Oh, I'm so glad you're here," she said, giving me a hug.

Also in her eighties, with bright hazel eyes and high cheekbones that belie her age, my mother is a slim, energetic woman known for her many friends and her tendency to overdo it when it comes to volunteering. However, the biggest challenge she faced at present had nothing to do with that or with her own accumulating health problems (bad knee, heart trouble, high blood pressure, etc.), but rather with the man in the room across the hall, whose history of work-related accidents and hospitalizations (including a five-month stay in this very hospital the previous winter, the result of a broken leg and a nasty hospital-acquired infection) had pulled her out of a contented retirement and installed her as a full-time nurse and ranch overseer.

"How's he doing?" I asked, nodding at the open door.

"Not good, I'm afraid."

"What do you mean, 'not good'?"

"Well, he's out of it."

"Out of it?"

"Go in. You'll see."

As we stood talking, a nurse arrived with lunch, and we followed her into a dim room where my father lay on his back, right arm in a splint covered with bloody gauze, left leg hooked to a wheezing machine that caused it to bend at a 45-degree angle every twenty or thirty seconds. His unshaven face was covered in bruises and cuts, and when he opened his eyes, bloodshot from lack of rest, I sensed a darting uncertainty there.

"Hello, sleepyhead," my mother said, pushing my father's gray hair back from his damp forehead. "Do you know who this is?"

"Rob," my father said in a rough whisper.

"That's right. He's come all the way from Indiana to see you."

He nodded slowly, his eyes tracking me.

After checking my father's vital signs, the nurse left us, and I watched as my mother spooned cut-up Salisbury steak and mashed potatoes into my father's mouth. When he'd finished those, she started in on the green beans and chocolate pudding, pausing every minute or so to give him a drink of syrupy coffee.

"Well, he's still got his appetite," I observed.

"Yes," my mother said. "There is that."

The meal over, my mother wiped my father's face with a washcloth and motioned me into the hallway.

"Since you're here, I'm gonna go back to the motel and lie down for a few minutes. Is that all right?"

"Of course," I said. "Go get some rest. You look exhausted."

"You have no idea," she said with a sigh. "But it's your father I'm worried about. I've never seen him so out of it. All the other times, at least he was right in his head."

"Go get some sleep," I said. "We can talk later."

I stood watching as she padded down the hallway in the direction of the elevator, oversized purse slung over her thin shoulder and gripped tightly with both hands.

As soon as I got back to his room, my father had a job for me.

"Rob! Is that you?"

"Yes," I said, coming up to his bedside. "What is it?"

"Shut that motor down."

I looked around the half-lit room with its blinking monitors.

"What motor?"

"The motor. Shut her down."

I looked down at the foot of the bed, where the machine I'd noticed earlier moved my father's left leg up and down.

"You mean this?" I asked, pointing to the device.

He nodded. "Shut her down. Get to going."

"I don't know," I said. "I'll have to ask the nurse if it's okay."

"Fine. Get to going."

I went into the hallway and told the nurse who'd brought the lunch about my father's request.

"Sure thing," she said, coming out from behind the nurses' station. "But we'll have to turn it back on in ten minutes or so. The doctor wants to keep that leg moving so blood clots won't have a chance to form."

We went back into the room, and I watched as she flipped a red switch on a little white box at the foot of the bed. The machine wheezed to a halt.

"Is that better?" the nurse asked.

My father nodded, eyes closed.

But as soon as the nurse had left the room, his eyes came open again.

"Rob?"

"I'm right here."

"Turn her on. Sixty percent."

"What?" I asked. "I just turned it off."

"Turn her on. Sixty percent. Get to going."

I walked back out to the nurses' station.

"He says he wants it back on."

"Okay," the nurse said, without looking up from her paperwork. "The switch is at the foot of the bed. Go ahead and turn it on."

I did as I was told, and the machine came immediately to life, raising my father's knee into a 45-degree angle before allowing it to straighten out once more.

"Shut her down," my father said.

"What are you talking about?" I said. "I just turned it back on."

"Get to going. You want to burn her up?"

"Burn what up?"

"The motor!"

Only then did I begin to understand. The "motor" he kept talking about was not the machine hooked to his leg but rather one of the ten or eleven irrigation motors we used to tend like slaves back on that farm west of Dodge City. The "Rob" he kept calling out to was not the fifty-year-old professor I was today but the fifteen-year-old boy I'd been all those summers ago. Finally, in his mind if nowhere else, my father was not a bedridden octogenarian with a badly broken body but rather a vital (if highly stressed) forty-something farmer with hundreds of thousands of dollars in loans to pay back and no rain at all in the forecast.

"Well, what are you waiting for?" he asked. "Get to going."

"Okay, I'm on it," I said without moving. "You can quit worrying about those sprinklers."

Looking back, I tend to see the five summers I spent working for my father on that farm north of Howell as an absurdist drama involving ceaseless toil and the witnessing of certain titanic struggles with fate in which my father played the part of Sisyphus rolling his rock up the side of a mountain, only to see it roll down again once he reached the top. That's a bit overblown, perhaps, but it neatly captures what it felt like to work eighty, ninety, a hundred hours a week in pursuit of a dream that could be wiped out by a failed irrigation motor or a single angry storm.

During one of those fateful summers—it may have been the first, when I was just twelve years old and my brother Joe was seventeen or eighteen—we spent the better part of a month trying to coax a couple of water-drive irrigation sprinklers into service in a field of drought-stricken corn. Day after day we toiled on the rusty sprinklers as well as on the motors supplying the water. Then, just when we thought we had the situation well in hand, we drove out to the farm to check on the sprinklers and found to our horror that one of them had twisted itself into a giant pretzel. Seven hundred gallons of water a minute shot like a geyser from the broken pipe. Looking at the sight from our place in the road, we saw rainbows. Rainbows!

Isn't that a little much? I wondered. *What's next? Being swallowed whole by a whale?*

"Well, I guess you'd better go shut her down," my father said, before beginning a slow, head-down walk into the field to inspect the damage.

That's the way he always reacted, but for my part, I hated to see it. Why didn't he rant and rave a little bit or, better yet, raise his fist to curse the gods? That's what I wanted to do, but somehow this response simply wasn't in my father. Instead, he reacted with a stoicism I found hard to understand. It troubled me that he *just stood there and took it,* as I thought of it at the time. I couldn't understand why he refused to quit when the writing was so clearly on the wall.

All these years later, I still fail to comprehend it.

As I made my way to my father's room at Manor of the Plains, I passed a series of "shadow boxes"—framed collections of words and images meant to tell the story of the resident outside whose room they hung. The first of these boxes featured a picture of an older man and his wife, a football flying through the air, and a cartoon image of a combine harvesting some unidentifiable crop. At the center top of the box was the man's name and the words "Career in Farming" and "Favorites . . . Sports." Center bottom were the words "I have seven children."

I was immediately struck by the similarities between this man's life and my father's. Everything claimed as individual in the man's shadow box could just as easily have been said of my father, who also loved sports and had seven children in addition to a career in farming and ranching. The words and images on the shadow box revealed several important facts about the man in the room, but they didn't begin to tell his *story.* Indeed, I found myself with more questions than answers. Who made the shadow box? Who was its intended audience?

Was the posting of these facts an attempt to stave off forgetting? If so, whose forgetting? The farmer's? His family's? That of his caretakers at Manor of the Plains?

These were compelling questions, but they couldn't delay my real purpose in standing in that hallway. I took a deep breath and crossed the threshold into my father's room.

He sat in a wheelchair, his back to me, head listing slightly to the left, as though trying to turn to see who was coming up to him from behind. For some reason, this small detail moved me powerfully. It reminded me of the way my mother had gripped her purse with both hands on her way to the elevator in Wichita. More than this, it reminded me of the image of my father stopped at the highway crossing at Howell, struggling to crane his arthritic neck far enough so that he could make out the traffic bearing down on him from both directions.

"How's it going?" I asked, stepping around my father's chair so that his eyes could dart up to take me in.

"Fine," he said in a weak voice. "How are you?"

"I'm good. I walked over from the house and had a hell of a time finding the right door."

He nodded slowly. "What time is it?"

I looked at my watch. "Eleven-fifteen."

"Almost lunchtime. Your mother will be along directly. Have a seat."

I moved a newspaper out of the way and sat down in a chair opposite him. The tiny room was crammed with furniture—bed, bookcase/dresser, flat-screen TV—and my father's wheelchair made it feel even smaller. Still, it was a nice room, better than what I'd been expecting. Before the place became Manor of the Plains, it had been the site of St. Mary of the Plains, the small Catholic college, now defunct, where my parents had met in the early 1950s. Before that, it was a dormitory for an order of Catholic nuns who raised my father from his birth to an unwed mother at the height of the Great Depression until his adoption by a German Catholic farm family who lived a mile to the west. How much of that complex history could be fit into the shadow box I imagined one of my father's caretakers hanging outside his room? "I was a Depression-era orphan." "I played fullback for the St. Mary of the Plains Cavaliers." What cartoonish image would they select to illustrate that life? Sisyphus pushing his boulder up the side of a mountain? The fleshy face of Winston Churchill, cigar jutting defiantly from his mouth? *Never give in, never give in, never, never, never. . . .*

But those were my ideas, not theirs—and probably not his, either.

We sat talking for ten or fifteen minutes, my father holding forth on the state of the World Series (the Royals were going to win in six), then offering an abbreviated report on the ranch. "Joe's coming in from Kansas City tonight," he said. "I guess the plan is to round up the cows tomorrow morning and get the calves worked."

"I know," I said. "I'm part of the plan."

"Joe called you?"

I nodded.

"Ah, good. It always helps to have an extra hand."

The whole time we talked, I was waiting for him to trip up and become the confused, angry person he'd been in Wichita. *Get to going! What are you waiting for?* It didn't happen. Evidently the swelling in his brain had subsided, leaving him with a better idea of what decade it was and who occupied the Oval Office.

However, the rest of him was still a wreck. Two months after the accident, he couldn't stand, couldn't walk, couldn't use his hands to feed himself or to hold a cell phone. All he could do was propel himself backward in his wheelchair with his one good leg, the way an infant scoots on its butt across a kitchen floor.

At eleven-thirty sharp, my mother arrived.

"Are we ready for lunch?"

"Ready," my father said.

On the way to the cafeteria, we passed the shadow boxes of two residents I'd known during my teen years. The first belonged to an assistant coach from my high school football team ("I have five children." "Favorites: Steak, Fishing, Hunting, K-State."), the second to a brilliant, energetic woman who'd taught biology at the community college when I was a student there ("I was a college professor." "Fa-vorites: Fruit & Coffee, All Flowers, Horses, Reading Mysteries."). In my mind's eye, I could see both of these people in their prime, the fiery coach yelling instructions to the offensive or defensive line, the teacher holding me and the rest of the lecture hall spellbound with descriptions of cell division mixed with tales of growing up on the East Coast, far from the world we inhabited.

At lunch, which consisted of Sloppy Joes, green beans, and lemon cream pie, the football coach wheeled up to our table and asked if I'd seen the beating the Oklahoma Sooners had put on the K-State Wild-cats the previous Saturday.

"No," I said. "But I think I heard the score on the radio."

The man looked at me with gleaming eyes. "I'm from Oklahoma City," he said, nodding slowly. "Did you know that?"

"No, I didn't," I said.

"I am," he said, nodding slowly. "From Oklahoma City."

Then he wheeled away from us and back to his table. Sitting next to him was a striking woman with strawberry blonde hair I slowly came to recognize as a cheerleader from my days on the high school bas-ketball team. We nodded at each other slowly. It was not our shared past that connected us in that moment but rather our shared present.

The next morning, I met up with my brother Joe and three hired cow-boys on my parents' cattle ranch fourteen miles northeast of town. For several reasons, all of them having to do with my father's prolonged absences, the ranch was in terrible shape. Fences were down, equip-ment lay about in various states of disrepair, and a broken faucet had been allowed to flood the northeast corner of the corrals, so that the pen where we usually kept the horses looked like a small, fenced-in lake. As for the cattle, they'd had to fend for themselves, crossing po-rous fence lines in search of better grass, drinking water from creek beds or wherever else they happened to come upon it. Obviously, none of this was the way a ranch was supposed to be run, but with my father laid up for months on end, and his hired man distracted by his uncertain future on the place, there didn't seem to be much that any of us could do besides help out when we were able to and hope that at some point our father would come to his senses and rent the place to someone younger and better able to take care of it.

While the hired man drove the feed truck out to the main herd, the rest of us saddled horses and fanned out across the ankle-high grass in search of stragglers and strays. It was a beautiful morning: blue skies, 46 degrees, no wind to speak of. In my group of riders was my brother Joe, a Kansas City lawyer and the de facto boss of the operation, and Dave McCollum, a professor of animal science at Dodge City Community College. It felt good to be on a horse again after months sitting behind a desk in the city. But this feeling was tempered by the fact that we came upon one dead cow after another. Some of them had been dead for weeks and were little more than bones and twisted hide. Others had died more recently and were only half-eaten by the coyotes and buzzards that would return as soon as we were gone. I kept a running total in my head, and at one point the inventory of dead reached six, along with a seventh, a lame cow that clearly wouldn't last much longer.

"What's the deal with all these dead cows?" I asked Dave.

"Dunno," he said, shaking his head. "Could be they got into some bad feed. Then again, maybe they're just old. Your dad tends to hang onto cows a little longer than the next guy."

"That's an understatement," I said. "They have to up and quit him, because he sure as hell isn't quitting them."

"Ain't that the truth," Dave agreed with a laugh.

In the far southwest corner of the ranch, we looked off into the distance to see a small herd of cows and calves that had slipped through the fence to graze in a neighbor's pasture a couple of miles to the south. After we'd brought the main herd in, Dave and Joe and I circled back to collect these escapees. In spite of the somber tone of my earlier thoughts, I enjoyed this work immensely, and I knew that Dave and Joe did, too. There's nothing like doing ranch work from the back of a good horse on a clear, cool morning. It's really not work at all. Nothing that satisfying is or could be. Even as I hoped that my father would retire and give my mother the break she deserved, I understood why he found it so difficult to do so. Ranch work was his life. If that ended, then what?

As the sun continued to rise, we gathered the last of the renegade cattle and loose-herded them before us in the direction of the corrals.

"Hey, you know who I saw at Manor of the Plains yesterday?" I asked Dave.

"Who?"

I rattled off the name of my former biology teacher from the community college.

"Really?" Dave said. "Golly, it seems like yesterday I was eating cake at her retirement party."

A couple of minutes ticked by during which the only sound was the cattle moving through the tall grass and the swishing of our horses' tails.

"Well, on second thought, I guess that party was eight or nine years ago," Dave continued. "Maybe even ten. I guess we'd better get busy living. What do you think?"

"I think you're right," I said.

We spent the rest of the day branding calves and culling cows. Joe sat on an upside-down bucket, a three-ring binder in his lap, keeping track of which cows were carrying a new calf and which were barren. If a cow wasn't bred, or was thin, or had marginal teeth, off she went to the sale barn. And the longer the culling went on, the more ruthless Joe and the vet became in their assessments.

"Gosh dang," the hired guy said at one point. "Seems like we're culling half the herd."

"That's because we are," Joe said with a shrug.

That evening, I carried the three-ring binder with its record of new calves and culled cows to my father's room at Manor of the Plains. I found him sitting in his wheelchair, watching a rerun of *Sports Center* on ESPN.

"Turn that thing off," he said as I came in.

I picked up the channel selector and pressed the off button, then took a seat in the chair across from him.

"How did it go?" he asked.

"Okay," I said. "The calves looked good. There were some really big ones, that's for sure."

"Well, those should've been worked in the spring," he said with a shrug. "With everything else going on, we never got around to it."

I had to smile at the understatement, so characteristic of my father. The "everything else" he threw out so lightly included a near-amputation of his right leg and a MRSA infection so bad he'd be on antibiotics for the rest of his life.

"What about the cows?" he asked.

"Not as good. Six or seven dead, and we had to cull quite a few old ones."

"How many is quite a few?"

"I don't know, thirty-five or forty. It's all in here."

I held out the three-ring binder, but he just nodded at a stack of mail on the bed, and I lay it there among the accumulating bills and bank statements.

I sat there expecting him to issue some grim assessment of the situation—his declining health, the sorry state of the ranch, the way the odds against him ever getting out of that wheelchair were slowly piling up. But the complaint never came. Instead, he smiled weakly and said, "Thanks for all your help. We couldn't have got her done without you."

"It's nothing," I said.

A silence fell between us. To extinguish it, I asked him what he remembered about when I came to visit him in the critical care unit in Wichita.

"Nothing," he replied.

"Really? Nothing at all?"

He shrugged.

"Well, it was pretty interesting."

"How so?"

"The whole time I was there, you thought it was 1978 or '79. You kept telling me to go shut down the irrigation motor. *Get to going. What the hell are you waiting for?* It was like we were on that farm north of Howell all over again. Nothing going the way we wanted it to. The corn burning up right before our eyes."

"Now that I do remember," he laughed.

"Yeah? What do you remember?"

He looked at me then with his tired, bloodshot eyes.

"Well, I remember that you were out there with me every summer. I remember how seriously you took the job. If I told you to run get a wrench out of the pickup, you always did just that. No questions or looking back. Just *run run run,* all the way to the pickup and all the way back."

We both laughed at the memory of that fifteen-year-old me.

"You know," he added after a moment, "in spite of it all, we still managed to do really good with that place."

"You think so?"

"Why, of course. Just think a moment. Without all the corn we hauled off those circles, we never could've bought the ranch."

It was true what he was saying, though every last bit of it flew in the face of my own interpretation of those years.

But maybe that's the way with all of our important memories. We take the raw material of the past and use it to construct a story in the present. Maybe that's what my father had been up to in that hospital room in Wichita. In the bright, focusing light of his delirium, he'd relived the Howell years not as tragedy but as the story of a time he'd called out to his sons for help, and those sons had responded with a burst of speed—no questions or delay tactics, just *run run run.*

"Behold," reads the last line of the Old Testament, "I will send you Elijah, and he will turn the hearts of fathers to their children and the hearts of children to their fathers, lest I come and strike the land with a decree of utter destruction."

Looking into my father's eyes, imagining what the future likely held for him, I had to admit I liked his version of the past far better than my own.

Acknowledgments

Many people offered encouragement and feedback as I wrote and revised this book.

Among family, I'd first like to thank my parents, Bill and Patricia Rebein, and my brothers, David, Alan, Tom, Joe, Steve, and Paul. Although we're not allowed to choose the family we're born into, I've always felt like I won the lottery in this regard. In a similar vein, I'd like to thank my beautiful wife, Alyssa Chase, a fellow writer and artist who is also my first and best reader; my children, Ria and Jake Rebein, whose childhoods in Indiana and Kansas inspired the first telling of so many of these stories; and my mother-in-law, Andra Chase, who never failed to ask how the work was going, even when she had artistic endeavors of her own to see to.

Among friends and fellow writers, I'd like to thank Mary Obropta, Anne Williams, Benjamin Clay Jones, Joe Croker, Nick Gillespie, Jake Nichols, Adam Carter, Chris Schumerth, Meagan Lacy, Bryan Furuness, and Josh Green. Thanks also to my wonderful colleagues in the English Department at IUPUI, especially Hannah Haas, Karen Kovacik, Kyle Minor, Sarah Layden, Mitchell Douglas, Terry Kirts, Jim Powell, JJ Stenzoski, Megan Musgrave, Jane Schultz, Missy Dehn Kubitschek, Tere Molinder Hogue, Steve Fox, Scott Weeden, Mary Ann Cohen, and Thom Upton. Thanks also to Dean Thomas Davis of the IUPUI School of Liberal Arts, Bronwen Maxon of University Library, C. Thomas Lewis of the School of Informatics, and the students in my Fall 2016 Writing Creative Nonfiction course. Each of you has encouraged me in some vital way, as have others I may have forgotten to mention here.

Finally, I'd like to thank my editor at the University Press of Kansas, Kim Hogeland, who believed in an early draft of this book, as well as Tom Averill of Washburn University and Jennifer Brice of Colgate University, who read and responded to the entire manuscript with insight and sensitivity.

Several of these essays were previously published, often in a very different form, in the following literary magazines and journals: "Why I Hate *The Wizard of Oz*" in *Booth*; "Bullet in the Brain" in *Yemassee*; "A Fire on the Moon" in *Ruminate*; "Of Cattle, Bush Hogs, and Men" in *Buffalo Spree*; "The Fight" in *Bayou*; "Hoops, Happiness, Pistol Pete, and Me" in *Georgetown Review*; and "Biscuits and Meth" in *Red Earth Review*. A special thanks to the editors of these journals, especially Robert Stapleton, Kristin Bussard, and Steve Carter, for their support and for permission to reprint these essays.

www.ingramcontent.com/pod-product-compliance
Lightning Source LLC
Chambersburg PA
CBHW050128030726
47505CB00007B/2086